Through Frankie's Eyes

Also by Barbara Techel

Frankie the Walk 'N Roll Dog

Frankie the Walk 'N Roll Therapy Dog
Visits Libby's House

Frankie the Walk 'N Roll Dog
Coloring and Paper Doll Activity Book

Through Frankie's Eyes

One woman's journey to her authentic self, and the dog on wheels who led the way

by Barbara Techel

Published by

Joyful Paw Prints Press
Elkhart Lake, Wisconsin

While the incidents in this book did happen, some of the names of some individuals and places have been changed. Any resulting resemblance to persons living or dead is entirely coincidental and unintentional.

While I refer to God in my book, it is not my intention for this to be about any particular religion, but rather about faith and trust. Feel free to substitute spirit, Universe, higher power, or whatever it is that you are most comfortable with.

Published in the United States by Joyful Paw Prints Press, Elkhart Lake, WI, joyfulpaws.com

Library of Congress Cataloging-in-Publication Data 2012920522

Interior photos:

- Barbara Techel
- Patricia Brunner, legacystudios.net (pages 11 and 165)
- Brook Burling (page 161)
- Lisa A. Lehmann, lehmannphotoart.com (page 175)

Editorial Supervision: Yvonne Perry
Copyeditor: Dana Micheli
Cover photograph: Brook Burling
Back cover author photograph: Lehmann Photography
Cover layout design: Derek Murphy
Interior layout: Caryn Newton

ISBN 978-09800052-9-5
PRINTED IN THE U.S.A.

What People Are Saying about Through Frankie's Eyes

A story of courage and compassion as one woman finds herself through loving partnership with her canine companions. Barbara's book offers inspiration for everyone who loves animals and desires to deepen in relationship with a beloved animal and with oneself.

– Dawn Baumann Brunke, author of *Animal Voices; Animal Voices, Animal Guides; Shapeshifting with our Animal Companions and Animal Teachings*, animalvoices.net

Through Frankie's Eyes *is a gorgeous tribute to the depth of relationship and connection that people can have with one another, themselves, domestic and wild animals and the Universe. Barbara's story is one of resiliency, allowing, perseverance, trust, faith and an immense amount of love. This book is guaranteed to bring your heart to a new level of loving, and will lift your spirit to higher ground. Barbara, you are an incredible inspiration!"*

– Sage Lewis, Author of *JAVA: The True Story of a Shelter Dog Who Rescued a Woman,* dancingporcupine.com

Through Frankie's Eyes *is a beautiful book about life, love, enlightenment, and lessons learned from a dog. The adage states the teacher appears when the student is ready. Frankie was the teacher, and Barbara the student... Through Frankie, Barbara's purpose found her.*

– Charmaine Hammond, Best-selling award-winning author *On Toby's Terms,* ontobysterms.com

In Through Frankie's Eyes *Barbara Techel searches for her purpose. Then, a little dachshund walks and rolls into her life, and shows her that purpose isn't necessarily what we plan, but the way we respond to what we're given. Through Barbara's honest account we learn to accept challenges gracefully, live happily, and to be more like Frankie!*

– Peggy Frezon, author of *Heart to Heart, Hand in Paw, and Dieting with My Dog,* peggyfrezon.com

As you read Through Frankie's Eyes *you will not only see the incredible love that can be shared by a person and a companion animal, but it will also become clear that they can shape our life in a positive way. Barbara Techel's inspiring journey unfolds as she describes how the dogs she was privileged to call family had a dramatic influence on overcoming some of her challenges and forging forward into the life she always cherished. The most remarkable aspect of this great book is the ability to place yourself into the story and find what you need to acquire the life and mission you want and deserve. Way to go Barbara and Frankie!*

– Joe Dwyer, author and motivational speaker, shelbysgrace.com

Reading Barbara's book I enjoyed learning about her path to finding Frankie and their mission in life. Their journey together to help others is inspirational and uplifting. The stories of her work with hospice and children is heartwarming, especially the chapter about Jackson. It felt like I was reliving that day as if I was there when Frankie and Jackson first met. It is obvious that Frankie continues to guide Barbara along her path to helping others.

– Linda Stowe, Founder of Dodgerslist, dodgerslist.com

Whether it's with our animal friends or humans, love is the door, upon opening, where we can meet our authentic self. This exceptional woman, Barbara Techel, gives the reader tears and laughter as she honestly reveals who she was, is, and is working toward, encouraging each of us to find our essential self.

– Lynne Carol Austin, author, lynnecarolaustin.com

Barbara Techel's moving story of her journey toward living a fully realized life, as inspired by a small dog who changed her life in ways she never could have dreamed

of, is an inspiration for anyone who is on a path of creating a life of purpose and meaning.

– Ingrid King, award-winning author of *Buckley's Story: Lessons from a Feline Master Teacher* and *Purrs of Wisdom: Conscious Living, Feline Style,* consciouscat.com

What seemed like a tragedy became a new beginning as Barbara Techel discovered the depth of her little dog's amazing spirit. Frankie showed Barbara how to keep rolling under the most challenging circumstances and led Barbara to discover her own true calling. Frankie and Barbara's amazing true story is full of heart; a must read for anyone who has been touched by a dog (or wants to be).

– Jenny Pavlovic, author of *8 State Hurricane Kate: The Journey and Legacy of a Katrina Cattle Dog* and the *Not Without My Dog Resource and Record Book,* 8statekate.net

Barbara Techel's memoir of her journey with her disabled dog Frankie is an honest and inspiring tale of a woman whose life was transformed by meeting a life challenge. We often wonder what our true calling in life is, while all the time life is calling to us giving us opportunities to achieve our highest potential. And that highest potential is always to love and be of use to others in their journey. When Barbara's six year old dachshund became paralyzed due to disc disease, she struggled with her own fears of what people would think of her and her little dog in a wheelchair. She struggled with her own feelings about disability and whether she wanted to meet the challenge of caring for a disabled dog. In the end, she found a deeper connection with herself, her dog and her community—realizing her dream of being a writer by sharing her story with others. This is a story of how being of service to those beings we love, we come to find our higher destiny.

– Leslie Grinell, Owner of Eddie's Wheels, eddieswheels.com

Barbara Techel does not shy away from the challenges of having a differently-abled dog. She dives into the fear and comes out a transformed woman, discovering on the way that her wheeling dog is an angel!

– Asia Voight, America's Animal Communication Expert, AsiaVoight.com

Table of Contents

Dedication

To Frankie.
My little sweetheart who showed me hope and faith
when mine was truly tested.

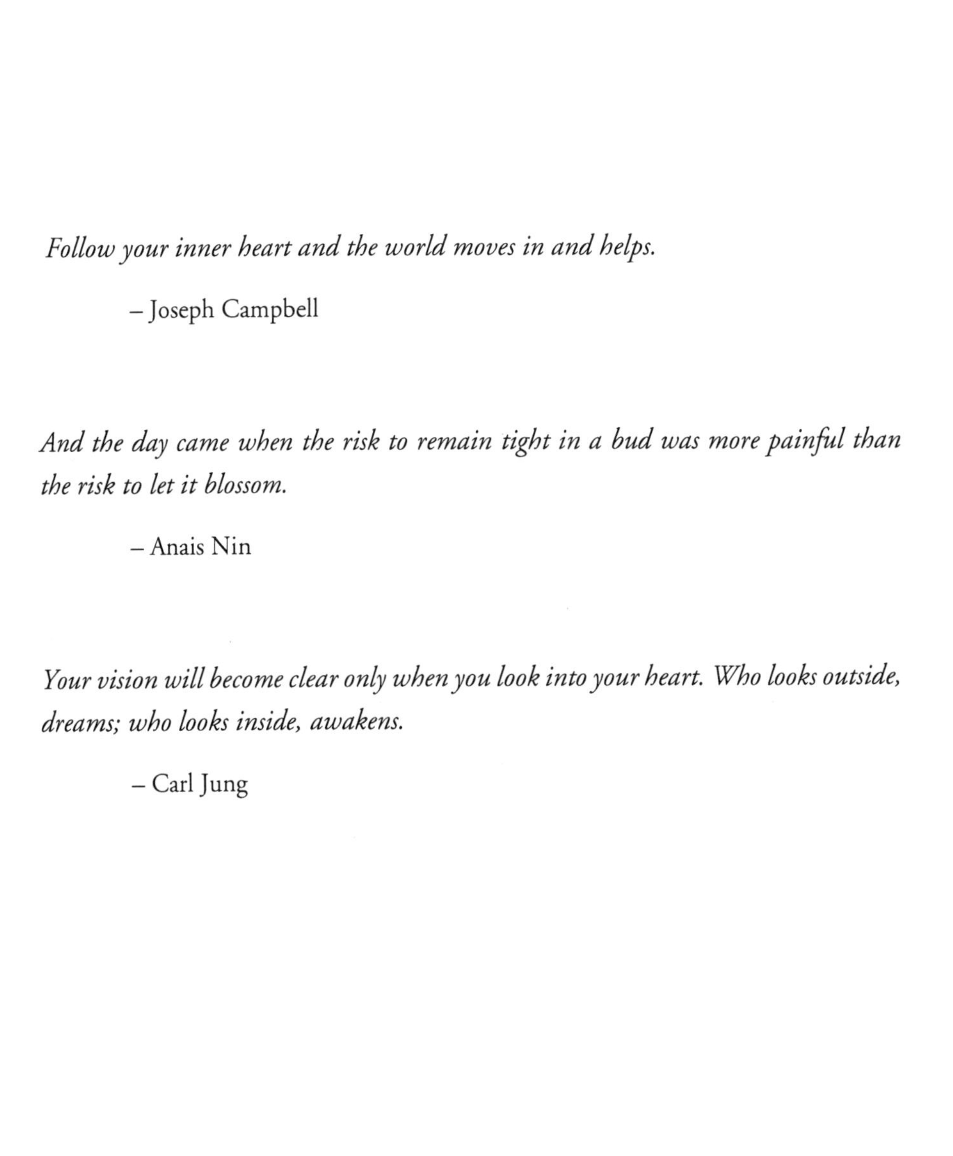

Follow your inner heart and the world moves in and helps.

– Joseph Campbell

And the day came when the risk to remain tight in a bud was more painful than the risk to let it blossom.

– Anais Nin

Your vision will become clear only when you look into your heart. Who looks outside, dreams; who looks inside, awakens.

– Carl Jung

Foreword

When Barb asked me to write this Foreword, I said yes, thinking I was doing a favor for a friend I admire and whose work I enjoy. I had no idea that reading her manuscript was going to change my life.

As I read the words I knew she had struggled to write—pushing through difficult memories and her fear of laying it all out there for the world to see—her engaging style made me forget I was reading for a reason. I just relaxed into the absorbing story of a woman discovering who she was and learning to embrace the person she found inside.

Of course, for me—an avid animal lover and advocate—the story was only enhanced by the presence of her dogs woven throughout the narrative. You can hardly keep from smiling-or crying when reading about Cassie, Kylie and Frankie. But it was watching Barb become more self-aware, progressively taking more control over her own life instead of allowing herself to be ruled by the opinions of others, that ultimately changed me.

Just as she grappled with her need to be who she really is and live an authentic life, I was facing my own crossroads. Like Barb, I was trying to reinvent my professional life. I had been struggling for years after the poor economy and technical advancements brought an end to the way I used to make my living.

But those things weren't the real obstacles to a positive future: it was my fear. Fear of having to learn new skills; of having to walk away from the comfort of the work life I'd built for myself and had enjoyed immensely; of having to admit that the way it had been was never going to be again.

I've never considered myself a fearful person. In fact, some people would describe me as frequently foolhardy or something of an adrenaline junkie. But the fact is, I was scared of my future. And just like Barb, I didn't have the luxury of waiting it out. I needed to make some kind of decision and get back into the game so I could move forward as a solvent, responsible, tax-paying citizen. But I didn't want to settle for just anything. I needed another vocation that would interest and engage me while allowing me to help people do better for themselves.

There's an ancient saying that, "When the student is ready, the teacher appears." It requires only that the student acknowledge her/his need to learn, and recognize the teacher when s/he appears. This book came along at just the right time, with just the right message I needed to hear. After flailing about for answers, I was very much in student mode at the time, and suddenly, there on my screen, the teacher appeared.

To say that I'm grateful for the insight and motivation *Through Frankie's Eyes* has provided would be the worst kind of understatement. I believe I'll look back on the decisions I've made since finishing this book as nothing short of a landmark in my career. And I can only wish for you the same kind of moving reading experience, whatever point you've reached in your personal growth.

One thing I can say for sure: if you've picked up this book, it's because you know you need something to inspire and uplift...so don't put it down. Hold onto it, read it, carry it with you, even after you've finished, for it will remind you that yes, you have work to do, but you absolutely can achieve the goals you're striving for. When necessary, refer back to the passages that most moved you (and I dare you to pick just one).

This is no lightweight puff piece: It's a testament torn from the gut of a woman who's overcome a great deal to learn what it means to live with integrity and intent. And it is a gift if you're open to accepting it. Let this story seep into your consciousness and inspire you—indeed, ALLOW you—to start or continue on your own fulfilling journey to who you really are. Like the very best furry little pal you've ever had, I believe you'll find it a worthy traveling companion.

Mary A. Shafer, Author/Publisher, *Almost Perfect: Disabled Pets and the People Who Love Them,* maryshafer.com

CHAPTER ONE

Bad Timing

I found a lump. It was roughly the size of a quarter. It felt somewhat soft, but also hard. *Was this always here?* I wondered. *How come I never noticed it before?* I tried not to panic, but worry immediately flooded my mind.

I sat down in my favorite oversized maroon chair, which has always made me feel safe and comforted at the end of a day. Typically, I would peruse my favorite country magazines or read a book while sipping a glass of wine or tea. Frankie, our red dachshund, would be curled up on the pillow next to me, sound asleep. Some days, I would gaze out the front door into the yard and smile as I watched my husband, John, play ball with Cassie, our chocolate Labrador. But on this sunny November day I just sat there, struggling to keep my mind from racing. What could this newly discovered lump be? I looked at Cassie's sweet brown face as she sat in front of me; then reached out to pet the top of her soft head. After a few moments of petting she lay down at my feet. I felt my heart warm with overwhelming love for my dogs as I soaked in their sweetness.

This was bad timing, I thought. Not that there was *ever* a good time to find a lump, but this was especially bad. I was studying to become a nutriceutical consultant and was about to take an important test that I desperately wanted to pass. It would enable me to work with doctors to educate and supply them with high-quality supplements for their patients.

Being healthy and in shape was something that I've always been interested in, though in my twenties and thirties I did many things that would not qualify as healthy. I weighed myself every single day. I wanted to see a certain number on the scale and if that number went above the ideal weight I had set in my head, I'd spend a horrible day berating myself. One way of keeping my weight in check was to skip meals, which I did for many years. John and I, newly married, would often go out on the weekends and party. Oftentimes I didn't know when to stop, and given the fact my stomach was usually empty, I would be sick the next day. Eventually, there came a point where I just got tired of getting sick. My new choice to keep my weight in check was to exercise excessively. Every morning, seven days a week, I worked out on my treadmill, followed by weight lifting. If I ate a piece of cake or something else I considered "fattening," I'd come home and work out again. I couldn't stand the thought of those calories being in my body. My whole life revolved around that number on the scale. It was a miserable way to live; there was a constant battle going on inside me to make sure I always looked my best. I wasn't considered bulimic or anorexic, but if there had been a name for what I was doing, my picture would have been next to the definition in the encyclopedia!

I don't exactly recall when my exercise obsession started to diminish, but it was somewhere in my late thirties. One day I just made my mind up that I'd rather be healthy than skinny. I wanted to enjoy life more, instead of constantly worrying. I still weighed myself, but I only did so once a week. I was kinder to myself if I gained a pound or two. Being healthy meant feeling good, and I began to understand it was not about a number. I made up a motto that helped me focus whenever I found myself wanting to slip back into old patterns: "Nothing feels as good as healthy feels." My new routine still included working out, but I cut back to five or six days a week. I also took vitamins and ate as well as I could.

During my second year of college where I was studying for a degree in fashion merchandising and marketing, I landed a part-time job working for Kohl's Department Store. I was thrilled when within six months, a full-time position for a visual merchandiser opened up. It was perfect timing— I was graduating soon—and an excellent fit for my degree. After interviewing for the job, I was so happy to be offered the position.

My job as visual merchandiser was to dress the mannequins in the latest fashions, as well as to merchandise the floor layouts each season for all the various departments. I worked there for twelve years. Sometimes I think I'd still be there if it wasn't for the last manager I worked for. He'd often take credit for the work I had done when the big honchos came for their quarterly visits. I didn't have the courage to confront him, so I put up with it for a year before I quit.

Though I was sad to leave a job I enjoyed, I was yearning to work closer to home. I also wanted to be more involved with my community. John and I had lived in our small town for close to ten years and I still didn't feel like I belonged. When I learned that a new resort was opening in town, I jumped at the chance. I applied for a job, and within a few days I was offered the position of sales coordinator. Essentially, this meant I was part of the sales team who worked on booking corporate events at the resort. It was my job to type up the contracts and coordinate extracurricular activities for the companies' employees. In the beginning, it was great fun to help open the resort. But there was also a lot of turnover, so there were some very trying times as well. However, I was able to purchase the car of my dreams—a shiny red Mitsubishi 3000 GT. I was so proud because it was a purchase I made with the money I had earned. I signed the loan on my own, without the help of my husband. I felt like this car was my way of showing others I had made it, that I was now a success in the way society defines it: sports cars and many other material things. This new job also got me more involved in the community. I participated in the monthly Chamber of Commerce meetings, and I was getting to know people in my town, which I really enjoyed. But after about three years, the corporate world and the inevitable politics that accompanied it had me frazzled. I no longer wanted to work at the resort. I wanted a simpler life.

John has a natural ability for remodeling and building. In the mid-1990s, he followed his dream of having his own construction company. Our plan was that he would get the business up and running and I would eventually join him in the office to handle the administrative duties. A year later, I was able to quit my job at the resort and work from home for John's business. Making the decision to leave my full time job was not easy at first. I worried that if we didn't find enough construction work, our finances wouldn't be stable. I was used to having a steady income and my own money to spend as I chose. We didn't have children, lived in a modest home, and didn't live outside of our means, yet it was still a risk to leave the security of my job.

To make the transition easier on us financially, we decided it would be best for me to find a part-time job, along with working for John's business. I was excited when I learned that another construction business in the area was looking for an office assistant. The job entailed pretty much the same duties I was already doing for our business. After meeting with the owner and his wife, I was offered the job. I was on top of the world and felt so much joy that everything had fallen into place. Handling the books for construction companies was new to me, but I was a quick learner and eager to do my best. I found there were some things the other construction business did that I didn't agree with, but I was certainly happy to have a little extra income of my own. It was not my ideal job and I was in a happier mood when I didn't have to be there, but at the time I really didn't think much of it; I simply went to work and did my job. After all, that is what I had been conditioned to believe: you go to work (whether you are happy with it or not), and then "live your life" when you aren't working. When I came home I felt I could be happy, and be myself.

CHAPTER TWO

A Nagging Ache

I'll never forget the morning of September 11, 2001. I was working from home that day, and was alone when I learned that terrorists had flown two planes into the World Trade Center and another into the Pentagon. A fourth plane, its target unknown, had crashed into a field in Shanksville, Pennsylvania, killing everyone aboard. I remember sitting in front of the TV, terrified; I really thought the world was going to end. I desperately needed to talk to someone, but I wasn't able to get a hold of John. I called my mom, and although she tried to comfort me, she couldn't assure me all would be okay. No one knew if, and when, something more would happen. Mom and I talked a little more, said our *I love yous,* and hung up.

I was in shock and could not concentrate on working. Frankie was curled beside me on her pink pillow. She always hung out with me as I worked. Having her near me always made my days lighter, no matter what was going on. I picked her up, hugging her tight and telling her how much I loved her. But I wanted to be with Cassie too, and I found her in the bedroom, curled on the bed, oblivious to what was happening. I snuggled close to her, with Frankie still nestled in my arms. I tried to tell myself that everything would be fine. But I had never felt so scared and unsure about anything as I did in those moments. I thought our world would never be the same again. It was an eerie and lonely feeling.

Like millions of other people that day, I remained glued to the TV, watching the attack being played over and over again. Everyone was desperate for answers. Later that morning, John came walking through the back door, his face pale and slightly dazed. He looked as shocked as I felt.

With my voice shaking, I said, "What's happening?"

"I don't know," he said, "but this is not good."

We didn't say anything else, just hugged each other. Someone had deliberately attacked the United States, and thousands of lives were lost. We mourned their deaths, as well as our country's innocence.

Two days later, I returned to my part time job at the other construction business. When I arrived, I found an angry note the owner had left for me. He had found an error in the spreadsheet that detailed his expenses and income, which I maintained for him. It stung to read his strong words on the page. I was still reeling from the horror of 9/11 and feeling a new appreciation for how dear life truly is. I couldn't understand why he would leave a note like this, instead of talking to me face to face, and so soon after our country had been attacked. *How could he be so cold?* I thought.

I tried to figure out how the mistake occurred, but I couldn't think straight. I did know that I didn't feel it was right to respond to his lack of consideration with another note. So I called him and asked if we could talk about it. He agreed, and when he returned to the office we sat down to what I thought would be a discussion of how we could improve our procedure moving forward. However, as we spoke, I had the overwhelming feeling that he wanted me to leave, but didn't have the courage to fire me. I tried to reason with him, suggesting we look at new ways of doing the report to avoid future mistakes, but to no avail. He wouldn't listen. With my lip quivering, I felt I had no choice but to leave. My face felt so hot, and I was trying not to cry.

I said, "Okay, I guess I'll just get my things."

He didn't say a word as I walked out of his office.

I was so humiliated. It took everything in me not to burst into tears, but I refused to give him the satisfaction. I loaded my things into my car as fast as I could, then I got in, slammed the door, and sped off. Once I was safely away the tears finally came and I cried all the way home. I couldn't wait to hug my dogs and talk to John.

I've always had a strong work ethic. To be let go from a job was incredibly hard to deal with. More salt was added to my wound when I tried to claim unemployment a few weeks later. My former boss fought it, saying he didn't let me go, but that I had walked out. This only added to my feelings of inadequacy. I felt like a huge failure.

Interestingly enough, for the past year, I'd often questioned what it was I truly wanted for my life. I'd silently ask myself, "What does Barb want?" But I didn't know the answer. Losing this job only added fuel to the fire. What was this thing called life all about? *Was this all there really was?* Little did I know that being fired would be a blessing in disguise.

A few weeks later, as I slowly recovered from the shock of losing my job, I heard about a home-based business for a gourmet food company. I've always loved to cook, so I thought this would be fun and a great way to earn a little extra income. I was missing the money I had been spending on myself.

As a gourmet consultant, my job was to find people to host parties. This meant demonstrating the company's products at gatherings. It was challenging and not always my thing to ask people to book a party for me, but once I did a few parties, the word spread. I became quite busy with parties four or five nights a week, plus a few Saturdays. I enjoyed being a consultant and loved the company, but after about a year, I grew tired of being gone almost every night of the week. I am somewhat of a homebody, so I was really missing nights with Cassie, Frankie, and John. Plus, working for our business during the days was just getting to be too much, so I quit the gourmet food company.

I decided working for my husband's business was enough. I would find other avenues to personally fulfill me, I thought. The first six years of John's business were profitable, and we were happy; then things took a downturn. We had made some risky business choices that threatened our financial stability, and life became a rollercoaster. I wanted desperately to not feel so scared all the time. To make matters worse, John and I were not agreeing on things in the office and I began to feel miserable and resentful. I didn't want this to affect our marriage.

We often fought over money. We also fought because each of us was trying to run the business in the way we saw fit. I didn't always agree with John's approach, and we talked about the business issues quite often. Years before, we had set Wednesday nights aside to go out to dinner, leave our worries behind, and just enjoy each other's company. But now our business talk even began to invade our date nights. In fact, it was invading our every waking hour together, and at times it made me really angry. I also became increasingly sad that we were dealing with so many issues. This business was John's dream, but deep inside I knew this was not really my calling. On the other hand, watching him struggle was difficult and I wanted to help him to make his business better. I also wanted it to work because I loved being home. I didn't want to go back out into the corporate world. But the bottom line was that I didn't want to have to worry about money.

Oftentimes I would take a break during the work day to go walking with Cassie and Frankie. The fresh air put things back into perspective for me, and I knew I could get through anything as long as I had my dogs. Being with them always calmed me, but at other times I struggled to find peace.

I still had this nagging ache inside me; I was still wondering what I wanted for my life, and this feeling only intensified as John and I continued to struggle. But each time the thought drifted through my mind, I let it go. At times it seemed too much to deal with. How does one figure out what they truly want?

In the meantime, I did my best to roll with the ups and downs of construction business. I've always had a strong faith in God. I was trying hard to keep that faith. Still, I found myself questioning why He was not helping us. I've never been a person to go to church, because I don't believe you need to go to a building to have faith. I have my own way of talking with God. Every day I read a little booklet called *Daily Word.* This is my time with God. At times I would sit in awe at how the daily message seemed to be speaking directly to me. It always helped affirm that there is something bigger at work in the Universe. It also helped ease some of the discomfort I felt about going against society's expectations regarding religion.

For many years, one of my family members had a very hard time with the fact that my husband and I didn't go to church. She would try to convince us that we *needed* to go. She feared if we didn't, we might not go to heaven when we die. I got so angry whenever she mentioned church and her worries for us. I also found it hard to believe that a loving God would punish us if we didn't go to church. That just didn't make any sense to me.

After a while I learned to let it go and believe in what I believe in. But it wasn't easy.

Our financial situation hadn't improved, so it seemed like a dream come true when my neighbor invited me to attend a gathering for a marketing business. The company promised high-quality supplements to improve people's lives, and I immediately accepted. It was a powerful evening, with testimonials by people whose lives were actually saved by taking the products. I've always been interested in health and in doing my best to take care of myself, so this seemed like a perfect fit. It also promised the opportunity to make a lot of money. I could hardly contain my excitement as I told John about it. Looking back, I can see the skepticism on his face, but then, I was oblivious to it all. I was so convinced this would take away all our money worries.

I signed up immediately, plunking down my $400 "starter fee." It was a big chunk of money at the time, and using it left very little in our savings. But I was convinced that it was the answer to our many prayers. Over the next few months I learned more about the products, which I enjoyed. But I also realized that although it was not classified as a multi-level marketing company, I would need to recruit others into the business to keep income flowing in. Selling the products was not enough; I also had to build a team under me that would sell products. The idea of having to recruit others was not something that appealed to me, but I thought I could get past it. To learn this skill, I listened to tape after tape, all recommended by the company. The tapes were testimonials of how successful others were in recruiting people and making a living. One person said that you will get ninety-nine noes before you get a yes. The thought of all that rejection made me cringe inside, but I pushed forward, thinking perhaps a miracle would happen. Maybe I would be lucky and it would just *happen* that I would build a team.

But a year later, I still had not recruited anyone into the business, and I was beginning to wonder if it was right for me. But I felt so stupid for telling John that this was our ticket out of our financial conundrum. How could I tell him, after all the money and time I had invested, that I thought I might be wrong? I felt I had to keep trying, even though something in me knew this was not the answer. I stuffed those thoughts down, thinking they weren't valid. I also questioned what was wrong with me that I wasn't comfortable recruiting others or, for that matter, selling products to others.

When the company created a new division to sell supplements through doctor's offices, we had the opportunity to become what they called nutriceutical consultants. Again, I really thought this would be something I could do. If I could bring doctors onto my team, I could stand to make a great deal of money. In fact, it seemed like a no brainer: doctors want their patients to be healthy, the products made people healthy, so the doctors would buy into this company. I signed up for the program and couldn't wait to get started.

The following day I was on my way to a conference to learn more about becoming a nutriceutical consultant. There would be a big test at the end of the weekend. I never studied so hard for anything in my life. One of my fellow trainees was a nurse. She had taken the test a few weeks before, and told me to study very hard for it. I asked if she could give me an idea of the questions so I knew what to expect, and how to prepare. She couldn't, but she did say I needed to know about the products and how they worked. Given the fact that she was a nurse, I assumed the questions would revolve around what supplements to take for certain health issues. I did my best to learn all I could about how vitamins work in the body, but I was nervous. I've always been better at hands-on learning than memorizing, but I was determined to pass this test. That's when I found the ill-timed lump.

CHAPTER THREE
Feeling Different

I pushed aside the thought of the mysterious lump and planned to make an appointment first thing Monday morning to have it checked out. I tried telling myself everything would be just fine. I hugged Cassie and Frankie goodbye and told them I'd really miss them. I also hugged John and waved good bye to my cat, Dani, who was perched on the ledge that separated the kitchen from the living room.

Another team member who was also interested in becoming a consultant offered to drive to the weekend conference. She didn't seem as nervous as I did about taking the test; in fact, she told me that she hadn't studied all that much for it. Halfway into the trip I realized this was going to be a long weekend. She was not the most positive person. The ride was filled with her complaints about things that had not gone right in her life. Between her drama and my worries about the lump and the test, I had a terrible headache when we arrived at our hotel. Even though I was not feeling my best, I was still excited about the conference. The anticipation of becoming a nutriceutical consultant by the end of the weekend helped me look past all my other worries. I couldn't wait for the conference to begin.

The next day we rose early and headed off to the first session. I was filled with hope that I had finally found something that would not only fulfill me, but allow me to earn enough to solve our money worries. But as the morning moved into the afternoon, I began to get an uneasy feeling in my stomach. This wasn't what I thought the training was going to be about. As I studied in the days prior to the conference, I put my all into learning about vitamins and how they work with the body. I truly wanted to be effective in helping others. Many of the attendees had specific questions about how to best help clients with certain illnesses and what vitamins to take. I had similar questions. But it became clear to me that this was more about selling the products and money to be made. At one point, one of the instructors told us we were worrying too much about how to help potential clients. We needed to focus on how to sell the products! Filled with apprehension that this might be another waste of time, I wanted to run as fast as I could all the way home. But once again, I stuck it out, pushing aside what my heart was trying to tell me.

As crazy as it sounds, I still thought that I might be able to have a positive impact on people's lives. On the last afternoon of the conference we were handed the test and given an hour to complete it. None of the questions pertained to how we would instruct our clients to take specific products for specific issues. It was basic questions about the company and sales tactics. In the end, it was really quite a simple test. Anyone who listened even half-heartedly could have passed the test with flying colors. While part of me was relieved it wasn't hard to pass, another part of me was annoyed that my nurse friend had led me to believe it was about how vitamins worked. More importantly I knew, deep down, that this venture was not for me. But yet again, I quickly dismissed that thought.

I managed to remain optimistic as my fellow team member and I drove back from the conference. But as we neared home, thoughts of the lump crept right back into my mind. Soon it was all I could think about. I put aside my uneasy feelings about the weekend. All I wanted now was to get the lump examined. I started praying the results would be good news, for anything else would be unimaginable.

For most of my life I had struggled with feeling odd that I never wanted children. John felt the same way; yet for the first year of our marriage I still held onto the belief that I was *supposed* to have a child. I grew up in the 60s and 70s, when having kids was just what you did. You got married and society expected you would have children. I often felt that something was wrong with me, especially when I heard my sister and friends say that they always knew they wanted children. But I never had that feeling.

I remember my grandma asking me each and every time she saw me: "When are you going to have babies?"

I'd say, "Grandma, I don't know." She had raised four children and didn't understand why I didn't know if I wanted kids or not.

One day, when she had asked the same question yet again, I got brave. "Grandma," I said calmly, "John and I don't want to have children."

She still didn't understand, and continued to press me each time we got together. Finally, on a visit to my aunt and uncle's home, she asked me again. This time my voice was stronger when I said, "Grandma, I'm not going to have babies. Please don't ask me that again."

She never did ask again, but I felt guilty for having spoken to her in that tone of voice. I loved my grandma and loved spending time with her. But I wanted her to respect my feelings. I think, more than anything, I didn't want her to think I was a freak or weird for not having the urge to have children. It was something I struggled deeply with.

This struggle was never more glaringly obvious than the day my younger sister came over to tell me she was pregnant with her first child. I was so mixed up that I couldn't find it in my heart to react with joy. I don't really recall what I said to her, but I know I wasn't supportive. I realized after she left that I had deeply hurt her feelings. It was because I simply didn't know what I wanted for myself. I still had the thought in my head that being the oldest sibling, and having been married for three years, I was supposed to have the first grandchild. Another part of me was jealous, which *really* didn't make sense. But because I was so caught up in what society seemed to expect, my head was a mix of jumbled up emotions.

That all changed when I met the baby for the first time. Oh, how I fell in love with that little girl! My sister had another daughter about two years later and I fell in love with her too. I found great joy in being involved with my nieces' lives as they grew, and this must have shown, because I learned years later that they thought of me as the "fun aunt." I really enjoyed the times they stayed with me. I could spoil them rotten and then send them back home again. When my older niece first began to talk, she had a hard time pronouncing her Rs, so Barbie became Bobbie and I became Auntie Bobbie. I wore that title proudly, and still do to this day. Each Halloween, John and I joined my sister and her husband to take the girls trick-or-treating. I always loved Halloween as a child, so seeing my nieces dressed up and excited really warmed my heart. Still, I would always get a mysterious pang of sadness when we arrived at my sister's and saw all the little ones decked out in their costumes. I now know it was because I was still struggling with the feeling that there was something wrong with me because I didn't want children of my own.

CHAPTER FOUR

Cassie and Frankie

I had been married to John, my high school sweetheart, for ten years when I finally brought home the little chocolate Lab puppy that I had begged for during the previous nine years. This was the first dog I had owned in my married life, and I was ecstatic. We'd had cats throughout the years, and I loved every one of them dearly. But a little fluffy dog would need me in a different way than they did. Not that cats don't need us, but they can sometimes seem a bit more aloof and to themselves. Dogs will do anything to please you, and they want to be with you.

I had seen a newspaper ad that there were chocolate Lab puppies for sale in a nearby city. They weren't from a breeder, just a family that decided they wanted to breed their female and male dogs. There was a litter of ten, and when John and I went to their home to pick out our puppy, I chose the first one that came running up to me. I was sitting on the ground, smiling at all the puppies around me. I was in heaven. This little girl crawled right into my lap, and my heart melted. I believed it was fate that she chose me. Since then I've read that is *not* the best way to choose a pet, but I didn't know any better. I have also come to believe with all my heart that she was meant to be mine, but it would take many years to recognize the deep, spiritual reason she came into my life.

I had always loved the name Cassie and if I *had* had a daughter that would have been her name. I knew driving to pick out our new puppy, that Cassie was what I would call her.

Watching Cassie grow and experience life was a real joy. I had never felt love like this. She was well-behaved, too, except for the occasional events that we called "twinkle toes." That's when Cassie was sniffing away at something, then sniffed herself right out of our yard. When John went to retrieve her, she would wait until she was a little more than arm's length from him; then, standing as if on the tips of her toes, she would begin jaunting back home. It was comical, with John's face scrunched in frustration and Cassie looking up at him out of the corner of her eye, as if she was saying, "Catch me if you can!" I'd be watching through the kitchen window, and it never failed to make me smile.

Never having owned a puppy before and not knowing what to expect, the first year with Cassie was also frustrating. I never took her to puppy classes, and looking back, I wish I had. Like many young pups, she loved to wander, and it was very hard to catch her. I'd be a just few feet from her, begging her to please stay. Then, just as I reached out to grab her collar, she'd pick up a scent and scoot off once again. It wasn't long before I would run out of patience and start screaming at her, then eventually start crying and pleading with her to stay put. I was so upset with her for being naughty, not realizing she was really just being a dog, and this is what dogs do if you don't take the time to properly train them. I always felt bad afterward, and would hug and kiss her profusely, telling her I was sorry. Then I'd beat myself up for having been so hard on her. After all, she was just a puppy. In time, of course, she outgrew these antics, and life with Cassie settled into an easy routine of playing ball, taking walks, and hugging and kissing her every chance I got.

When Cassie was six years old I had this intense urge to bring home another dog. This time I had my heart set on a red, smooth dachshund, and it had to be a girl. I also had her name picked out long before I saw her. I've always thought it was so cool when a girl had a boy's name, and so I named my new dachshund Frankie, after the song Frankie and Johnny, from the 1900s. Frankie and Johnny were sweethearts in the song, and since I called my husband Johnnie, it seemed to fit.

Johnnie, however, couldn't understand why I wanted another dog, especially a dachshund, "Why do you want a wiener dog?" he asked.

"I don't know," I shrugged, "I just do. They're cute."

He rolled his eyes, and though I felt a bit guilty for forcing another dog on him when he clearly didn't want one, I couldn't let it go. That's how bad I wanted one. Without his blessing, I began my search for a breeder. It wasn't as easy as I thought it would be. I found many breeders in our area who bred long-haired dachshunds, but my heart was set on a red one, and what they called a "smooth-coat" dachshund.

One afternoon, on yet another Internet search, I finally located a breeder in Brooklyn, Wisconsin. It was about two hours from where we live. There was one little dachshund puppy from a recent litter that still needed a home. It just so happened to be a girl, and she was also a red smooth-coat. Again I thought, yes, this must be fate, and she is meant to be mine. When I first saw her picture on the computer screen, my heart grew ten times its size. I thought I had never seen anything so cute as her tiny little face with the long nose and a long body to match. But while I was thrilled that I had finally found her, I knew John was still not on board with my decision. So I made an appointment to just go *see* the puppy. Lori, my sister-in-law and a fellow animal lover, agreed to drive.

She picked me up early on a dreary Saturday morning in November. I met her at the back door with my purse already slung over my shoulder, eager to be on our way. "Aren't you going to bring a carrying kennel with you?" she asked.

I shook my head. "No, I'm just going to go see her and then decide."

Lori knew better and grinned. I tried hard not to grin back, because although I knew she was right, John was standing nearby and could hear our conversation. Still, it didn't take much convincing for me to take one along "just in case."

John watched as I walked to the car with Lori, the carrying kennel in my hand. "I thought you were just going to look."

Knowing full well I wasn't being one-hundred percent honest, I said, "I am." Then I quickly got into Lori's car before he could say anything more.

As we headed for Brooklyn, I was filled with anticipation of seeing this sweet little puppy. Still, I tried to convince myself that I really was just going to look. I know now that John didn't believe a word of it anyway. Over the years he has come to learn that I am a very determined woman when I want something; he knows when he will win a battle, and when he won't.

Two hours later, Lori and I arrived at the breeder. To the right of the long gravel driveway, there was a large fenced-in area with huge trees swaying in the wind. Inside, what looked to be over one hundred wiener dogs were romping about and barking up a storm. I giggled with delight when I saw all those short-legged dogs running back and forth. I felt like I was in dachshund heaven!

Rosalyn, the breeder, came out of the house and walked toward us. I introduced myself and Lori, then reiterated what I had said on the phone a few days before: I was just there to check the puppy out.

Smiling, she said, "Would you like me to bring her down so you can meet her?"

I nodded my head enthusiastically. "Yes."

She told us to wait, then disappeared back up the gravel driveway.

Lori and I stood near the car for what seemed like forever. The other dachshunds were still barking like crazy as they tried to figure out who we were. Then I glanced toward the top of the driveway and my heart stopped. Delicately prancing beside Rosalyn was the cutest little puppy I had ever seen! As they got closer, my eyes filled with tears. I couldn't get over how tiny and sweet this little one was. Lori was pretty smart. She knew there was no way I was going home without her.

As Rosalyn and the pup got closer, I knew I was a goner. She was about the size of a guinea pig, and as soon as she bounced jubilantly towards me, I scooped her up into my arms. She licked my face all over, and her tail was wagging a hundred miles a minute.

Rosalyn said, "I'll leave you with her for a few moments so you can get to know each other."

I nodded, but it wasn't necessary; I already knew I loved her, and I whispered as much into her tiny ear. I looked at Lori and said, "You were right. Who was I kidding when I said I was just coming here to look?"

We both laughed, then I looked at my new little love and said, "Would you like to come and live with me?" Her tail seemed to wag faster. I took that as a definite yes and said, "Okay, then, I'll take you home."

A few moments later, Rosalyn returned, a sly grin on her face. She hadn't been fooled either.

I said, "I know I said I was only coming to check her out, but I'd like to take her home today."

Her grin still in place, Roslyn told us she just needed to put in her microchip. I agreed; the microchip would help us locate her if she ever got lost, though I had no plans whatsoever of ever letting her out of my sight. She was just too precious.

It only took about ten minutes to insert the chip, then we followed Roslyn into her house to fill out the necessary paperwork. As soon as we walked in, we saw the dachshunds; they were curled up on the sofa, on rugs, on blankets, in dog beds, and just about everywhere I looked. Most of them, Rosalyn told me, were now elderly and retired from breeding, so she kept them in the house with her. I couldn't help but think how I would love to have all those doxies hanging around my home.

I felt a deep sense of peace as I held my new puppy in my arms. Once I signed the paperwork, I thanked Rosalyn; then Lori and I walked back to her car and I gently placed my precious little one in the carrying kennel. Lori folded the backseats down and we perched the kennel in between the passenger and driver's seat so she could see us. I was so tempted to hold her all the way home, but thought she would be safer in the kennel.

The whole way home, I kept turning around to look at my new bundle of joy. With her small face and big black soft eyes, she reminded me of a mouse. I told her that her name would be Frankie and she cocked her head to the side, looking at me as if she understood. I said, "You like your name, don't you?"

Except for getting sick once, she did really well. I was so happy to have her, but as we got closer to home I started thinking about John's reaction. I knew he was not going to be happy with me. Lori and I talked about this on the way home. I told her I thought he'd be a little angry, but would forgive me once he saw Frankie. He had never been one to stay upset for long. Either way, I was already so in love with the dog that there was no way I wasn't going to keep her.

When we pulled up to the house, John was outside with Cassie. I had to work hard not to grin, but I was bursting with excitement. I opened my car door and then the back door, and reached in for the kennel. I could feel John watching me.

When he saw Frankie in the kennel, he said, with a tinge of anger in his voice, "I thought you were going to just go look at her."

"I know, but look at her, she is just so cute. I couldn't leave her there."

He shook his head back and forth. I could tell by the look on his face he was indeed upset. I took her out of her kennel and set her on the lawn, which was in much need of cutting. Frankie nearly disappeared in the tall grass. John looked down at her, and with just the slightest upturn of one corner of his mouth, he said, "Your legs must be on back order, Frankie." I knew then that in no time at all he would adjust to having another dog in our home.

Cassie sniffed around Frankie for a minute or two. Then she went to lie down on the cement floor of the garage. I picked up Frankie and brought her over to Cassie.

"This is your new little sister."

She looked up at me with the whites of her eyes showing, as if to say, "Yup, I see her, but what am I supposed to do with her?"

I thought it might take a while for Cassie to warm up to her, but by the end of Sunday, they were snuggling up to each other like they had been best buddies forever. As for John, it didn't take long at all for Frankie to wiggle her way right into his heart.

CHAPTER FIVE

Difficult News

Though I was still uncertain as to whether being a nutriceutical consultant was truly right for me, I felt I needed to give it a chance because of the time and money I had invested. I also still had high hopes that I could earn enough to contribute to our challenging household finances. But before I could begin my new job, I needed to face the lump I had discovered the day before the conference. The lump was on Cassie's right hip and I prayed it was nothing serious.

Hoping to alleviate my worries, I talked about it with family and friends. Many assured me it was likely a fatty benign tumor, which a lot of dogs get. If this was the case, the lump could be easily removed. This helped a little bit, but I was still fearful. I felt the lump once again then picked up the phone to call the veterinarian's office. I sighed with relief when they gave us an appointment first thing the next morning.

The following day, Cassie jumped into the back of my car and we were off to the vet. I remember looking at her in the rearview mirror and thinking how very much I loved her. I tried telling myself everything was going to be just fine. It was probably as everyone had said, just a fatty tumor that could be removed, and life would continue as normal.

Cassie's vet, Dr. B, examined the lump. He said he didn't like the feel of it. He wanted to take an x-ray. I waited in the exam room for what seemed like an eternity, silently praying that all would be fine. Dr. B finally came back in the room.

"I'm sorry, he said, "but I don't have very good news."

Hot tears instantly filled my eyes. He put the x-ray up on the board and showed me the tumor. He explained that part of the tumor was pressing on Cassie's spine.

"I believe she may have osteosarcoma."

"What does that mean?"

"It's bone cancer."

"Can it be treated?" I asked, my voice shaking.

"Possibly, but in many cases it's terminal. I'm not positive it is cancer because Cassie's tumor is in an odd place. Typically this type of cancer is found on a forelimb, and in those cases if the cancer has not spread, the leg can be amputated. Dogs adjust very well to having three legs. We will need to do a needle biopsy, which will only take about ten minutes.

I choked out the word, okay, and he took Cassie to the back.

As I watched them walk away, I fervently began to pray again: *Please let this not be cancer.*

A few moments later Dr. B brought Cassie back out to me. "The biopsy is done. It will take about a week before we know the results." He handed me a brochure of a veterinarian teaching school in Madison. I briefly glanced at it. "There is still a possibility this isn't cancer. But if it is, you may want to consider taking Cassie to Madison to learn about the treatment options."

I put the brochure in my purse and hugged Cassie around the neck.

"I just know it won't be cancer."

Dr. B smiled. "I hope so."

As we drove back home, I looked in the rear view mirror to see Cassie's head resting on top of the seat between the head rests. Her big brown eyes looked right into mine and pulled at my heart strings. Even though I was trying to convince myself it wouldn't be cancer, I was still very scared. "I love you so much, girl," I said, the tears streaming down my face, "I'll do whatever it takes to help you."

Upon returning home we were greeted by Frankie, her tail wagging a hundred miles a minute. It always made me smile to see her so happy to see me. It also brought me some comfort. Frankie sniffed Cassie, as they always did when one returned after an absence from the house. Cassie took a big drink of water, then headed to our bedroom and hopped up onto the bed. Frankie was right behind her, climbing up the steps John had made so she could get onto the bed without having to be lifted by one of us. They snuggled together and before I knew it they were both fast asleep. I took the brochure out of my purse and briefly glanced at it before setting it aside. I didn't want to "jinx" the biopsy by thinking about the vet teaching school and the possibility of having to go there.

Thanksgiving was the last weekend of November that year. We celebrated the holiday with John's family. John's Dad said the family prayer before we started feasting on all the good food. I silently prayed and asked God once again to please let Cassie be okay.

A week had gone by and I still hadn't heard from Dr. B. My heart skipped a beat every time I heard the phone, but when it rang around 6 p.m. on Friday, I just knew this was the call. My heart was racing and my hands shaking as I picked up the phone. I was slightly surprised when I heard a woman's voice on the other end; Dr. B was not in the office that day, so his partner, Dr. C, was calling with the results.

As soon as I heard the words, "I'm so sorry to have to tell you this…" I began to feel lightheaded and as if I might get sick. Then the words I had dreaded all week sent my world into a tailspin, "but the results of Cassie's biopsy shows bone cancer."

I sat down at the kitchen table. My head dropped down and I let out a loud, screeching cry. I was absolutely devastated. My whole body began to shake. Looking back, I feel sorry for Dr. C, so helpless on the other end.

"I'm so sorry," she kept saying, "Are you okay?"

I finally managed to gather myself together. I told her I'd be okay and thanked her for calling. I hung up the phone and felt like nothing would ever be the same again.

I had almost forgotten John, who was standing next to me when I got the call. When I looked up at him, I saw he had tears rolling down his face too. Without a word, I stood up and we hugged each other tight.

After a few moments, John said, "What can we do for her?"

I picked up the brochure and handed it to him, "I'll need to make an appointment here."

The following morning I called the vet teaching school. When the receptionist answered, I explained that I had been referred by Dr. B, who had diagnosed my chocolate Lab with bone cancer."

"Oh, I am so sorry," the woman said, her voice full of sympathy, I waited a minute while she checked their availability.

"I have an opening this Thursday at 10 a.m."

"I'll take it." I said, dreading another week's wait for the appointment.

My friends and family again tried to tell me everything would be fine. We were all hopeful there would be a cure. Lori once again offered to drive me, and while I was grateful and relieved to have someone go with me, I didn't want Cassie to ride in an unfamiliar car. She understood and said she would drive my car. The teaching school was a little over two hours away. I couldn't help but think the last time we drove to the Madison area: the wonderful day I picked up little Frankie. Now my heart was heavy with worry, but we tried to stay positive and hope for the best. Lori kept reminding me that even though it was cancer there may be a way to treat it. I clung to her words and tried to not let despair creep into my mind.

When we arrived, Cassie was eager to get out and sniff around for a much needed potty break. When she was finished, I checked in with the receptionist and got the consultation fee out of the way. She told us to have a seat and that someone would be with us shortly. It didn't take long before we were brought to a room where a vet examined Cassie's lump. The young vet introduced herself, but my mind was so clouded with fear that I forgot her name the moment she said it. To this day, I can't even recall what she looked like, only that she had long blonde hair. But I do remember how kind she was. She was so gentle with Cassie, making her feel at ease with her soothing voice, approaching her slowly, and gently feeling the lump on Cassie's hip. After she was done with the examination, she began to talk with me about the options. Her biggest concern was the location of the tumor.

Echoing Dr. B's words the week before, she told me this type of cancer is found on dog's forelimb and usually requires amputation of the leg, followed by chemotherapy. Cassie's tumor, however, was in an odd location, and according to the x-rays, was touching her spine. Surgery would be risky.

"Will the chemotherapy make her sick, like it does humans?" I asked.

The vet shook her head. "Most dogs do very well with it and don't get sick. But even when owners choose amputation, or in Cassie's case, removal of the tumor, and chemo, it usually only adds another year of life."

When I heard those words I immediately felt sick to my stomach. I was also doing all I could to stop myself from bursting into tears. As she continued to talk, the pale yellow walls of the room felt like they were closing in around me. The closer the walls came, the more I saw nothing but black. Somehow, though, I was still able to hear what the vet was saying. "Because Cassie's tumor is in an unusual spot, to remove it would mean removing all of her leg, plus a large portion of her hip. It is also likely that we can't get the entire tumor."

The thought of disfiguring her like that was unbearable. "I can't do that to her, plus chemo, just to extend her life by a year."

She nodded, understanding my concern. "There is the possibility of radiation, but I can't guarantee that would work either. Another x-ray will help to determine the exact location of the tumor, and whether radiation is a viable option."

"Well, I would like to consider radiation, since it seems my only hope." I glanced over at Lori, who had come in with me for moral support. She nodded her head in agreement.

"Since we have to sedate her to keep her still, it will take about two hours. If you want to grab some lunch and return around 2 p.m., we will know more then."

My legs felt like noodles as I stood up. I don't remember walking out of the room, but I do remember seeing the vet walk with Cassie down the hall.

The next thing I remember was sitting in the passenger side of my car, my head in my hands as I sobbed. It all seemed so real now: my Cassie girl had very few options, and probably not much time left. The helplessness I felt was too much to bear.

Lori tried to comfort me. "We still may get some good news. Don't give up hope yet."

I tried my best to believe her.

We found a place nearby to eat lunch. I ordered a sandwich without even really thinking about it. I wasn't hungry. I just wanted to know the outcome of all this. The waiting was just too painful. I took tiny bites out of my sandwich and tried not to cry again.

To get my mind off things, I told Lori a funny story about Cassie. Two months earlier, John and I took Cassie and Frankie on vacation to a cabin four hours from home. We arrived after the long drive and John and I began unpacking our truck. Cassie stayed in the back seat as we went back and forth bringing things inside. On a trip back to the truck, we saw that Cassie had tried to climb to the front seat. The problem was her belly had gotten stuck, so now half of her was in the front and half was in the back. Her front feet dangling, and her body wobbling back and forth, she looked like a teeter totter. John and I laughed so hard we had tears running down our faces.

John took one look and said, "Oh, Humpy Lumpy." Well, that just made us laugh even harder!

Lori and I laughed now too, but this time the story made me burst into tears. It made me so sad to think that Cassie might not be around for more of those trips.

When we returned from lunch exactly at 2 p.m., a few moments later we were taken to another room to talk with the vet once again. She showed me the x-ray and confirmed that the tumor was indeed pressing on Cassie's spine. She then called in a second vet to corroborate what she saw. Both agreed that both radiation and amputation were too risky, because one wrong move could permanently paralyze her. As I realized that my two options to help Cassie were now completely out of the picture, I felt my heart sink to my feet. I couldn't even cry anymore.

I looked at Lori, then at the vets. "Is there nothing else I can do for her?"

"Well, there is a new experimental drug that seems to slow down the growth of tumors like Cassie's. It's not a cure, but it could give her a few more months to live."

The vet saw the look of hope return to my face, and made it very clear that this was not a guarantee.

"I can't tell you how long she'll have, but it might help. Without treatment, dogs with bone cancer typically pass away within four to eight weeks."

The drug was our only hope of having her with us a little longer. "I'd like to give it a try."

It was not that expensive— one hundred dollars a month-- but given our current situation, I wasn't sure how John and I would pay for it. It didn't matter; I had vowed to Cassie that I would do all I could to help her.

On the way home I called John with the news. I heard his sharp intake of breath when I gave him the prognosis. Then I told him about the drug.

"How much is it?" he asked.

"A hundred dollars a month."

John didn't hesitate. "Don't worry about the cost. We will make it work."

That helped ease my mind a little. I remember thinking that if I had to sell my red sports car, which I loved, I'd do it in a heartbeat to help Cassie. She was so much more important. I started her on the medication as soon as we got home.

When I met my mom two weeks later for lunch, we talked for a bit about what I had learned when I took Cassie to the teaching school. She then slid an envelope across the table to me. Inside was a lovely card and one hundred dollars. It has always been difficult for me to accept help from others. I want to be strong all on my own. Tears ran down my face as I said, "Mom, I can't accept this."

"Sometimes you have to let others help you, because those who love you feel helpless and want to help in any way that they can."

I knew she was right, even though it was hard for me to accept. But I also realized she needed to help. "Thank you," I said quietly and gratefully. She helped several more times in the next few months, and I learned to accept it graciously.

Cassie was diagnosed three weeks before Christmas, and I vowed to make her remaining time as happy as possible. I would be there for her no matter what. That Christmas season I hugged and kissed her more than I ever had before. She may have been thinking, "Gee, Mom, enough already!" But I just couldn't help it. I loved her so much. I also soaked in all the beautiful moments of her and Frankie hanging out together quietly, or doing their crazy-chase-dance around the living room. John and I got this dance going by clapping our hands until they got all wound up. Cassie would chase Frankie around the ottoman; then at some point, Frankie would spin her tiny body around and she would be doing the chasing. John and I would laugh and laugh. John also lovingly called them "The Twins," like the movie with Danny DeVito and Arnold Schwarzenegger.

CHAPTER SIX

What's My Purpose?

We rang in the New Year full of uncertainty, for I didn't know how long we would have Cassie with us. Around this time, something in me began to shift and I started to look at life differently. I intently observed how Cassie lived with cancer. She didn't realize she had cancer. She lived each day just as she had before the diagnosis. She was still happy and very much herself. This began an ache in me and had me wondering what I was here to do. I'd found myself looking at Cassie and thinking, what is this thing called life all about?

Suddenly, I realized how the first half of my life had flown by, and I was scared the second half would do the same. What would I have to show for it? I also felt like I had lost much of the joy I had years ago, but had no idea how to find that joy again. When I was let go from my part-time job at the construction company, I had felt something stirring in me, but I pushed it aside because it felt uncomfortable. At the time I thought I was struggling with feelings of inadequacy, but now I was having all these thoughts again. At first I attributed this to Cassie's cancer diagnosis, but I soon realized that the feeling was more intense this time. It was like I *had* to figure things out.

I knew I wanted to find a way to give back, as well as leave a legacy behind. The fact that I didn't have children and didn't plan to ever have them made me wonder, "If I died tomorrow, would people even know I was here?" It was scary to think I would die someday without leaving my mark on the world. I was also having many mixed feelings about the marketing business I was doing, especially after attending the conference in November. I knew in my heart it wasn't for me, yet I still felt like I had to give it a shot. Cassie's impending death reminded me daily that something was amiss in my life, yet more time would pass before I found the courage to face what my soul was trying to tell me.

I couldn't find any enthusiasm to work the business or find doctors with whom to share the program. The yearly conference was also approaching and I dreaded the thought of going. I didn't want to be away from Cassie, for I would never forgive myself if something happened to her while I was gone. As hard as this is for me to say without feeling some guilt around it, I was also actually relieved. It made it easier for me to let my team members above me know I wasn't going because of Cassie. Though I knew the real reason was that I wanted out of the business, I was too fearful to admit it. I always felt tremendous pressure to attend all the conferences and meetings. There were many times I simply didn't want to go, and now I wouldn't have to. I also decided to take a hiatus from the monthly meetings. It felt good to let that go as well. But it didn't help me to not feel like a failure. I couldn't bear the thought of telling John or my friends and family that I didn't want to continue with it. The battle going on inside my head was driving me crazy.

I still felt guilty about telling John that this business would solve all our financial worries. Yet a year later we were still struggling. I felt I had to keep trying, and in fact I was feeling pretty confident that I could bring on board my own doctor, Dr. M, whom I highly respected. I was thrilled when she agreed to an appointment so I could explain the program to her. My team leader, Carol, said she would go with me. I understood that Dr. M's time was very precious. Her patients came first, and I was going to honor that. When I arrived at Dr. M's office fifteen minutes before our appointment, I was surprised to find Carol already there.

"How long have you been here?" I asked.

"I got here about 10 a.m. to see if I could get in early to see Dr. M."

"Why?"

"Sometimes doctors will have a free moment in between appointments, so I thought I could talk with Dr. M then. But I didn't have any luck with that."

Carol could be more forward than I was. I was mad she had done this and felt she was crossing some boundaries, but I said nothing. On the other hand, a part of me admired her confidence.

A few moments later we all met in Dr. M's office. Carol took the lead, explaining the program to her. I barely got a word in edgewise. I didn't know whether it was my imagination, but I felt like Dr. M was uncomfortable and didn't want to buy into the program. When Carol pressed her for an answer, I wanted to run.

As turned out, I was right; Dr. M decided not to carry the supplements in her practice. While a part of me was disappointed, a huge part of me was relieved. I was so uncomfortable with the way the meeting had gone. I also realized I would have to approach other doctors I didn't know, and the thought made me more nervous than ever.

A few days later I put together a list of potential doctors I could cold call. As I sat at my desk, going through the phone book, my stomach twisted into knots. I was a nervous wreck and found myself in the bathroom several times before I picked up the phone. Maybe cold calling was just not my thing, I thought. How I managed to get another appointment with another doctor, I don't even know. But I did.

Carol checked in with me each week. When I told her I had an appointment with another doctor she said she would go with me. Again, I didn't have the courage to tell her no, and in all honestly, I just didn't have the guts to do this on my own. I tried convincing myself it would get easier.

The doctor Carol and I saw a few days later was not interested in the program. After that, I knew I couldn't do this anymore. I quietly bowed out of being a nutriceutical consultant. While it made me happy, I still felt so much guilt. I'd question myself over and over, "Why couldn't I do this business? What was wrong with me?" When I couldn't take any more of the banter going on inside my head, I'd go to Frankie and Cassie for a sense of peace. My dogs always made me feel grounded. I would feel the world lift off my shoulders whenever I took them on walks, or even just sat with them on the couch.

In addition to its nutriceutical consultant program, ABC Marketing Company had several other divisions. In late February the company announced a new weight loss program. Many people were experiencing success with the new weight loss supplements. I thought, *this is really it. I can do this!* Having always been interested in health and fitness, I was lulled once again into thinking I could bring people into the business by first helping them lose weight. I should have known better. In the end, it played out in the same fashion as the nutriceutical consultant position. The old knots in my stomach arose each time I had to introduce the weight loss program to someone. After about a month I was frustrated that no one seemed to be interested, and I once again wondered what I was doing wrong.

One day I called up my friend Joan and asked if I could stop by her house. I needed some advice about the business I was doing. I thought maybe she could help me figure out how to find people who wanted to try the weight loss program. I even thought that she might want to try it herself.

I met with her the next morning and explained the program. I told her how hard it was for me to find people willing to try it. For the first time, I didn't hold back; I told her that everything I tried just didn't seem to work.

She listened quietly for a while. Then she said, "I think you should call this lady I know. Her name is Diane and she's a life coach." Joan grabbed a pen and a piece of paper, wrote down the woman's website address, and handed it to me.

I had never heard of a life coach before. I was also a bit miffed that she thought this would help me. It was not the advice I was looking for. I had called her because I thought she could help steer me in the right direction, but instead I was being told to see some kind of therapist. I didn't see how a life coach was going to help me find clients to try this program.

"Thank you," I said, careful not to let my disappointment show.

I drove home, more annoyed and upset than ever. I wanted to quit the whole thing. Once again I beat myself up with thoughts like, "What's wrong with me? Why can't I make this business work?" I sat down in the living room, snuggled with Cassie and Frankie, and allowed the tears to flow.

When I finally stopped crying, I turned my attention more closely to my dogs. Cassie was doing well on the experimental drug, and as I looked at her now, I wondered whether she knew she had a terminal illness. I also wondered if Frankie knew Cassie was sick. It didn't seem that way. Cassie was still the same dog, eager to play ball and go for walks. I found myself thinking, why is it that dogs don't worry about things as we humans do? In this moment, I wanted to be Cassie or Frankie so I wouldn't have to worry anymore. Impossible, of course, but it was an appealing thought nonetheless. I also thought about the day Cassie would die. I wondered if I would know when it would be "time" to euthanize her, or if Cassie would die on her own once the cancer became too much for her body. I had no idea what to expect; the drug she was taking was experimental so we could only guess as to how long we would have her. The thought of her not being there was sometimes too hard to bear. It made me think about how I could find more joy in my own life. It wasn't that I was miserable; there were many things about my life that I loved. Yet there was an undeniable void that I couldn't explain. I kept wondering, *what is my purpose?* I knew there had to be something more and I wanted to discover it before my life passed me by.

The next day I couldn't stop thinking about the life coach Joan had told me about. Could she really help me? Maybe she could help me market the supplements to those who wanted to lose weight. I started to feel a little hopeful, even though I still had no idea what a life coach really did. I also wondered if she would even *want* to help me.

Finally, I decided to go to Diane's website to learn more about her. As her site came up on my screen, the first thing that caught my eye was the mission statement: "Serving business leaders who want to discover who they are, decide what's important, and do what matters...in business and in life." My heart fluttered a bit, and as I read on, I became quite fascinated with her services. A life coach, quite simply, was someone who helps you figure out what you want to do with your life. Well that certainly was something I was struggling with. *Could this be the answer I was looking for?*

I was definitely curious, but my mind immediately went to cost. I had no idea what she charged, and our finances were tight because I had spent so much money on various programs with the marketing business. I wasn't sure I could justify spending more money on something that was not a guarantee, but as I read the statement again and again, it continued to resonate with me. It helped give me the confidence to contact Diane.

I began by writing her an email to introduce myself and explain that I needed help with my business. Specifically, I was trying to find clients for the weight loss program I represented and was interested in learning more about marketing. Diane emailed me back the following day, saying it would be best if we spoke over the phone. I agreed, and we set it up for two days later at 11 a.m.

It was a warm day in early April when I made the call to Diane. My heart was beating fast. Asking for help was so hard for me, but I knew I had to try. I was so tired of feeling like a failure, and that was enough to make me pick up the phone.

My hands were shaking as I punched her number on the keypad. As I heard phone ringing on the other end, I sat down at the kitchen table and looked out my front door. Cassie was lying under the maple tree, watching the world go by. It was her favorite spot to be and it always made me smile to see her there. Looking at her now helped me feel more at ease. Cassie had reminded me once again that life is short and that we must grab the opportunities presented to us.

Still, my stomach was in knots when Diane answered. We began by talking about the marketing business I was engaged in. I reiterated that I thought I needed help in finding clients. I also gave her a little bit of my background and my previous job history. As I grew more comfortable with her, I brought up my struggle to find what really makes me happy. In particular, that I had trouble reconciling my definition of success with society's version. Finally, I confided that I wasn't sure the marketing business was for me and my feelings of inadequacy.

As I told her my story, it struck me that I had been lost for quite some time. In my senior year of high school, there was huge pressure put upon students to decide what they were going to do with their lives. We were constantly asked what we planned to major in at college and whether this was the "right" choice. Looking back, I was happy with my decision to pursue a degree in fashion merchandising. I also truly enjoyed my job as visual merchandiser at Kohl's department store, which I had for many years. But no one tells you that it's okay to change your mind, and try new things as you grow and evolve. That's why I berated myself so for jumping from job to job; I thought there was something wrong with me, that I couldn't stick with anything.

After our discussion, Diane said, "I'll write up a proposal outlining how I see us working together and how I can help you. I will include a couple of different options, as well as costs for each. I'll have that to you in the next few days."

"That sounds great. I'll look forward to what you come up with."

As our conversation came to a close, I was excited and enthused, and tried not to worry about the fee. I sat there for a few moments, thinking about the ideas we had exchanged, and suddenly I felt the intuitive part of me take over. I just *knew* if I worked with her, I would come to feel better about myself. I knew I wanted to take this step. I was ready for a change.

CHAPTER SEVEN

Digging Deeper

Patience has not always been one of my strongest virtues, so waiting for Diane's proposal was hard. As promised, she emailed within a few days. It was expensive, but I still felt confident that she could help me. I knew I had to find a way to make it work, but first I had to share my plans with John.

I'm very fortunate to have a husband who has, for the most part, been open to listening to me. When I told him about Diane and my hopes that she could help me, he supported the idea. He knew how unhappy I had been. I told him what it would cost, then added, "I'm willing to do whatever it takes to cut down on other expenses."

"If you feel this will help you, then we can make it work. Don't worry about the money."

I started to cry as I hugged him. What a gift he had just given me… and what a gift I was about to give myself.

I immediately emailed Diane to let her know I wanted to move forward. She said the next step would be to decide how often I wanted to meet with her. I also had to let her know if I wanted to meet in person or by phone. Coaching is often done by phone, but I felt I needed to meet in person.

A week later, I hopped on my bike and set out on the one-mile ride to Diane's home. I was nervous about our first session, but excited as well. I knew she only took on clients who were serious about making changes, and I was determined to do so, even though I knew this meant I'd have to dig deep into my soul. I knew I'd have to speak my truth and most importantly, trust in my truth. I was ready.

Diane is a warm and gracious lady and I felt instantly welcome when she greeted me at the door of her cottage-style home. We chatted briefly for a few moments, then she said, "My office is above our garage. If you're ready, follow me."

We walked outside to the garage and made our way up a narrow flight of stairs. The office was quaint and cozy, with a floral-patterned sofa. She invited me to sit down and offered me a cup of tea, which I thought was lovely.

"I call it my tree house," she said when I complimented her on the décor.

It overlooked the lake and was absolutely divine. I was envious of the space she had to call her very own. It had a peaceful quality that made me feel safe. I couldn't help but think it was a perfect place for me to start digging into my soul.

Our first session lasted three hours. Typically, a first coaching session lasts only about an hour, but there was a natural flow between us. I felt comfortable with her, and although I surprised myself by opening up as much as I did, I knew I wanted more. That day, I committed myself to three months of coaching.

As I rode my bike back home, I felt this huge weight lift from my shoulders. As I peddled, I made a conscious decision to pay close attention to my thoughts and feelings, and to enjoy the process. This was a time just for me. A time I carved out to discover who I really am. I wanted to bring more joy back into my life and I was willing to do what it took to do just that.

In a follow-up email the next day, Diane gave me some fieldwork to complete before the next time we met. This included keeping a journal of the various thoughts and concerns that popped into my mind as I went through the coaching process. She said I could send her emails of those thoughts or keep them to myself, whichever I was more comfortable with. She also sent me a values worksheet that I needed to complete and fax back to her.

Another item on my list was to write a letter to my former boss at the construction company. In my first session with Diane I had shared the story of how he had let me go and how I felt about it. She encouraged me to tell him how I perceived the situation, and tell him my side of the story about the error in the spreadsheet. I needed to tell him how he hurt me and that his actions left residual feelings that had affected me all this time. She said to tell him that I have moved on and would no longer let the situation haunt me or get in my way. She also encouraged me to forgive him. I initially had a hard time with this, but Diane said that while I didn't need to tell him, I should try to forgive him in my heart.

Once the letter was complete, she suggested a ritual that would help me put the situation behind me. I could burn the letter, bury it, or seal it in an envelope and tuck it far away. Lastly, she asked that I send her an occasional note or call her to let her know what was working, what wasn't, and what might be too time-consuming. I was still a bit scared of what all this work might reveal and how it could potentially change my life, but Diane reassured me that the process should be something that I embrace, find exciting, and empowering. She stated that though we would cover tough issues, it should not feel burdensome or overwhelming.

The thing I had to tackle first was the letter to my former boss. I didn't want that hanging over my head anymore and I didn't want it to stop me from moving forward with the other assignments. At first I didn't understand how this could be effective, since I wouldn't be sharing my actual thoughts with him. But as I wrote the letter, I actually felt it cleansing my wounded soul. The more I wrote, the freer I felt. I was amazed at the impact of how liberating it was to express my feelings on paper. After all this time, I finally realized it was okay that I was let go. It didn't mean I was a failure; it simply meant that I was being given an opportunity to allow a new adventure to come into my life.

After I finished writing the letter, it was time to decide on what ritual I would use to release it. I welcomed the idea of burning the letter. Burying it or sealing it in an envelope meant those feelings could still exist and potentially come back to haunt me. Burning it meant I'd never have to see evidence of those feelings again. They would burn into ash and the wind would scatter them out into the Universe. That felt right to me.

I read it to John first. It was healing for me to say the words out loud, and although I cried a little, it helped to cleanse my soul even more. When I was done, we walked out to our backyard and John started a fire in our fire pit.

With a light and grateful heart, I forgave my former boss and released my negative feelings to the fire. I would no longer give any of my energy to him. I could now move forward with my dreams and figure out what I wanted just for me.

My next task was to work on my values worksheet. I enjoyed taking the time to really evaluate my values for the first time. I had to rate each value on a scale from one to five, five being essential and one, not so important. I couldn't have more than five "essentials" and no more than ten that I considered "very important." My top five values, in order of importance, were job tranquility, knowledge, help society, location, and moral fulfillment.

I recalled that when I left my full time job, I knew without a doubt I no longer wanted to be in the corporate world. It was too hectic and fast-paced for me, so the fact that I chose job tranquility as a priority seemed fitting. Another value, knowledge, intrigued me. "Engage myself in pursuit of knowledge, truth, and understanding." After some thought, I realized this resonated with me as well, for I was seeking my own truth.

The meaning of the value, "help society" also struck a place deep inside me. I didn't know how I could help society, but I knew I wanted to explore that more. I had a feeling it might go a long way to filling the void inside me.

The meaning of "location" was more straightforward: "work in a place that is conducive to my lifestyle; a desirable home base for my leisure, learning, and work life." For the past few years I had worked from home while helping John with the construction business, and I had always enjoyed it. I also thought Diane's tree house was lovely, and I dreamt of having something like that of my own someday.

The last value, "moral fulfillment," was defined as "feeling that my work is contributing to ideas that I value as being important in the larger context." This one seemed to go hand in hand with my desire to help society. Thinking about the two values together made my heart flutter, even though I still had no idea as what direction I was headed in.

Next, I had to take these values and work on a forced values exercise. Doing this would help me narrow down what I wanted to do with my life in terms of work, volunteerism, and personal fulfillment. I examined my current jobs, working part time for John and the marketing business, listing advantages and disadvantages of both. Then I listed other ideas that interested me, whether it was something that I got paid for, doing volunteer work, or staying home.

I believe women tend to have many interests; at least, that's what I've gathered from talking with friends. My sister-in-law often kidded me about all the different things I wanted to do. For example, my list included working at a bookstore or library, being a dog walker or animal communicator, working at a flower shop, helping people decorate their homes, volunteering with my dogs ...the list went on and on. No matter what path I decided to explore, I knew that I wanted to wake up every morning, eager to start the day.

In my next coaching session, I learned that narrowing down my choices wasn't going to be easy. I became very frustrated when I looked at all the Post-it™ notes Diane had stuck to the dry erase board on her wall. Each one listed an area of interest of mine.

To help me hone in on what was truly important to me, Diane drew the shape of a pie and divided it into sections. I had to fill out each section of the pie with something I considered important. Doing this, Diane said, would help me see what brought me joy and how I could live my life in balance. I must admit that at first I didn't see how this exercise was useful.

One of the things I had listed was that I wanted to explore being a writer. When we first started exchanging emails Diane had commented that I expressed myself beautifully in writing. It's always been easier for me to write out my feelings than to verbalize them. I also enjoyed writing in middle school and high school, and I had even filled an entire notebook with poems written for John. My friends had also commented on how easily I expressed myself through my writing. They often said that I write from the heart, and some even said I should write for Hallmark! It was a high compliment, though I never took them seriously. In my forced values worksheet I only listed one disadvantage to being a writer. I thought it could potentially be lonely. However, I certainly liked its advantages: location (I could write from home or in a café), flexibility, tranquility, and the potential for creative expression, and independence.

I had often discussed with Diane my love of animals, especially dogs. In part, at least, it was because of Cassie's cancer and her impending death. But even beyond that, I'd loved animals for as I long as I could remember. I have a picture of myself at two years old, holding a little tiger-striped kitty. His name was Tiger, and when I looked at the picture, my little arms wrapped around his tiny body, I know that this is when my deep love of animals began.

As I began to narrow down my choices, keeping in mind my pie graph of my "importants," dogs and writing seemed to fit nicely into the mix. I was relieved to have made it through the forced values exercise with some measure of success and excited to explore the dog-writing avenue. Diane suggested that perhaps I could write about dogs for magazines or newspapers, and I liked the idea. She suggested I interview an editor to see what I would need to know in order to do that. Diane also said I might want to consider writing a children's book; maybe a book about dealing with the death of a pet, since I was facing the impending loss of Cassie. Initially, I was excited about the idea, but then became too nervous; I didn't think I had what it takes to write a children's book.

I did, however, move forward with the newspaper idea. I happened to know the editor of our local paper; she was my friend, Joan, the one who referred me to Diane. I contacted her and asked if we could get together for lunch. I told her I was interested in asking her some questions about the paper and how one goes about writing for it. Two days later we met at a local café. I told Joan that I had taken her advice and hired Diane as my coach. She smiled, and said she was pleased to hear how well things were going.

"Well, one of the things I am exploring is becoming a writer. My ideal subject would be writing about animals, especially dogs. I'm really passionate about sharing with others what animals teach us."

Joan nodded in the affirmative. "I could see you writing about animals because I know how much you love them."

"How does a newspaper work? I mean, how do you find writers and decide what goes into a paper?"

"Well, each month I'm on the lookout for various local stories. When I get a lead, I call that person up and ask for an interview. Once the interview is complete I come back to my office and write the story. I'm also responsible for soliciting ads, which helps pay for the printing of the paper. Once I have all the stories written, along with photos and ads, I then begin laying out the paper."

"Wow," I said, "there sure is a lot that goes into putting a paper together."

"Yes, there is. In fact, I had thought about the idea of having a monthly column in the paper dedicated to stories about animals. But I just can't seem to find the time to write it."

My mind began to race. I thought, Oh! How I'd love to have my own column and write stories about animals. But I was too scared to say anything because I didn't have any experience.

But a few moments later, it was as if a light bulb went on above Joan's head and she said, "How would you like to write the stories? You could have your own column."

"I'd love to!"

"It doesn't pay much- only ten dollars a story."

"I don't care about the money. I just want the opportunity to write about animals."

I was so happy to be given this opportunity and thanked Joan several times. I remember reading somewhere that when you are excited and nervous all at the same time you're on the right path. This was certainly what I was feeling in this moment, and I was thrilled.

As happy as I was to know I would be writing for the paper, I also began to realize how much I was struggling with being a part of John's business. I felt obligated for many reasons. I also felt guilty because, after all, it was what I *thought* I wanted years before. Diane coached me to gently and compassionately share with John my hopes and dreams for myself.

I started setting more time aside for my writing and pursuing other avenues. As I continued my coaching process with Diane, I began to see that asking for help is not a weakness, but a gift. Once I accepted that, it seemed other things in my life started to fall into place. I realized I was building character and becoming a stronger person.

One day, Diane said, "You are not a failure for trying so many things in life, but rather someone who is an explorer. Look at all that you have accomplished."

I really pondered those thoughts and took them to heart. What a refreshing way to look at it. It made me feel so much lighter, and even proud of myself. I was an explorer, not a failure!

I now know that working with Diane was one of the best things I've ever done for myself. How often do we stop to think about what really matters to us? I believe that if everyone took the time to do their own soul work, it would have a profound and positive effect on our world. How often do we tell eighteen- or nineteen-year-olds that they should know what they want to do with the rest of their lives? We urge them to go to college, get a degree, and stay in that field forever. I've heard parents insist their children go to college because they themselves didn't but wished they had. While I realize parents want the very best for their children, I also wonder if there is a better way to encourage the younger generations to explore what they are most passionate about.

Coaching opened me up to looking at life more from my heart and less from my head. I couldn't help but think how refreshing it would be if we could encourage high school graduates to do the same; teach them that opportunities and circumstances in their lives may change, but that by following their heart and their authenticity they will live a more joyful and purposeful life. After all, isn't that what we are all seeking? The key is to believe with all our hearts that we are worthy and have much to offer this world.

In essence, that was the most important thing I learned through coaching: I matter. I've also learned that it's of great service to me to listen to my heart. When I do, I find myself living with more joy and purpose, which reflects back into the world in a positive way.

CHAPTER EIGHT

Saying Goodbye

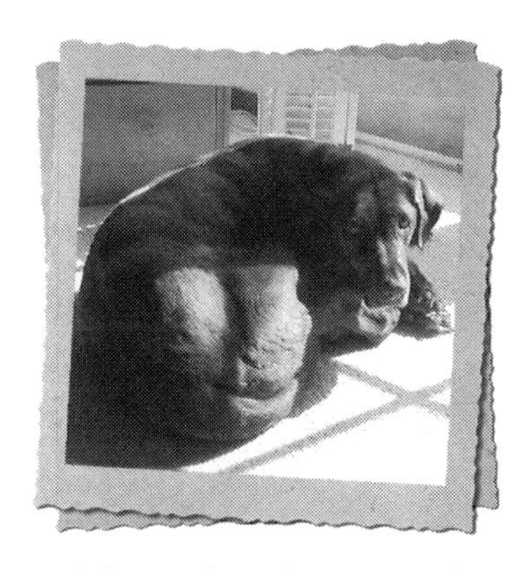

My first story for the newspaper appeared in the July 2005 issue. I named my monthly column, "For the Love of Animals." The title of my first article was "Quality of Life." I wrote about how difficult it is when our pets are diagnosed with a terminal illness. I shared with the readers the heartbreaking results of Cassie's diagnosis, and the limited choices I had to help her. From all I had experienced and learned in the past eight months, I had come to the conclusion that the determining factor in making medical decisions for your pet was quality of life. Once the quality of Cassie's life had deteriorated, I knew I would need to help her cross over. When I sent my article to Joan for publication, I requested that it be dedicated to Cassie.

Two weeks before my story went to print and one week before my forty-first birthday, Cassie began to show signs that the cancer was taking over her body. The tumor, which started out the size of a walnut, had grown to the size of a grapefruit. The week before, I had taken her to the vet because she was licking her back end excessively. I was also finding spots of urine around the house. After examining Cassie, Dr. B explained to me that the tumor was now pressing against her bladder. This was causing her to leak urine.

He said, "I think you might want to start thinking about euthanizing her."

Though I knew there was no cure, that this day would eventually come, all the pain came flooding back. We'd had eight months together since her diagnosis, and while I continued to hope for a miracle, I was always aware of the elephant in the room. Now that elephant was staring me down. We were about to have to make one of the hardest decisions of our lives, and I thought my heart would break into a million pieces.

"I need to think about this and talk to John," I told the vet.

"Of course, take your time. I understand."

Of course, John was devastated as well. We decided to watch Cassie closely over the weekend, and by Friday morning she refused to eat when I set her kibble down. I tried not to be too concerned; there was always dinner. But again, she refused my offer of food. On Saturday morning I watched Frankie gobble up her breakfast, praying with all my heart that Cassie would do the same. But she wouldn't eat. I cooked up some chicken and beef, thinking it would entice her, but she only sniffed it, looked up at me, and laid her head back down. I'd heard that when dogs stop eating, it's their way of letting you know they are dying. Her breathing had become quite labored over the past two days, and several times I found her sitting in a corner, staring at the wall and breathing heavily. She had never done that before. I tried to pretend it wasn't happening, but in my head I knew it was time. I just couldn't bear to think about the end.

How was I going to live each day without her? She was my heart, and through her illness, she helped me to get help with my own life. How could I ever thank her? I recalled an article I had read on the Internet, about cancer in dogs. There was a theory that animals take on humans' stress and that it's a possible cause of cancer. I thought about all the stress in our household the past few years. Had it given Cassie cancer? The guilt I felt was overwhelming.

That afternoon, I had some heartbreaking discussions with John, my mom, and Lori, and in the end it became clear: as difficult as it was for me to face, we had to do what was necessary to ease Cassie's suffering.

That evening, I sat outside with the dogs while John made chicken on the grill for dinner. Tears spilled down my cheeks as I gently petted Cassie's head. Frankie was nearby, lying in the grass, quiet and calm as a little church mouse. She watched every move I made, as if she knew what was going on. It was so excruciatingly painful. I wished I could turn back the clock and have more time with her. Looking back, I wish I had enjoyed these last moments with her, recalling all the joy she brought me, instead of being so lost in her impending death.

Cassie hung out in the garage as John and I ate dinner and cleaned off the table. When it was time to turn in for the night, I stood by the screen door and called Cassie to come in. She looked back at me with her big brown eyes, and then looked away. I called her again, but she kept staring straight ahead. I walked out to her and said, "Come on girl, time for bed."

But she refused to come in, which she had never done before. I walked back inside and called her name once more. She still wouldn't get up. My heart fell to my feet when I realized that this was another sign I had read about: when animals are dying, they sometimes want to be alone so as not to upset their owners. I knew I had to respect her wishes, but it was so heartbreaking. I got a sleeping bag and laid it out on the garage floor so she had something soft to lie on; then I put her on a long lead and attached it inside the garage so she couldn't wander from the yard. It was warm that night, so I left the overhead door open. I set her bowl of food and water next to her in case she decided she wanted to eat, then sat down next to her and wrapped my arms around her neck. My tears soaked her fur as I told her how much I loved her. Then, finally, I walked into the house and headed to bed.

Frankie snuggled next to me as I tried, unsuccessfully, to fall asleep. I got up several times during the night to check on Cassie, and was relieved each time she raised her head to look at me. If she didn't look up, I walked over to her to make sure her stomach was still rising and falling. I felt so torn, for as much as I didn't want her to die, a part of me hoped she would die on her own. I dreaded having to make that call to the vet the next day. Both thoughts filled my heart with pain. There was no easy away around this.

When we awoke on Sunday morning, Cassie was still with us. As happy as I was to see her sweet face, John and I both knew it was time. Letting her go was the most humane thing we could do. She again refused to eat and she still didn't want to come inside the house. I left her food in the garage in case she changed her mind. She laid under the tree for most of the day and her breathing grew progressively more labored. We also noticed that when she walked she wasn't putting any pressure on her back leg. I knew she was probably in a lot of pain. This brought me to tears again. I knew I had to make the call.

My hands were shaking as I picked up the phone. Since it was Sunday and the vet's office was closed, I called Dot, a friend of mine who works there as a vet technician. After explaining what had been happening with Cassie all weekend, I took a deep breath and said, "We've decided it's time. We would like to bring her in first thing tomorrow morning."

"I'll take care of everything—plan on arriving around 8 a.m."

I began to cry again, and Dot told me how sorry she was.

Making the appointment to euthanize Cassie was one of the hardest things I've ever had to do, but part of me was relieved too. I felt like I was helping Cassie and that made my heart a bit lighter.

That night, I sat outside with Cassie, still unable to believe it was our last night together. Somehow, through the tears, I found the courage to take a snippet of her fur as a keepsake.

Through all of this, Frankie hung out with us too. I wondered if she knew Cassie was dying, and how she would deal with Cassie not being there to snuggle and hang out with. I worried that she'd be lost without her best buddy.

On Monday morning it seemed like a thick cloud of sadness was hanging in the air. The night had seemed to drag on forever, which in a way I wanted, but in another way I didn't.

Lori had asked me the day before if she could stop over before work and say goodbye to Cassie.

"Of course," I'd said, touched by her offer, "I think she'd like that."

Now, as she walked in the kitchen door, we didn't say anything to each other. There just were no words. She knelt down in front of Cassie, who was lying on the floor, and petted the top of her head, whispering goodbye. Cassie lifted her paw and placed it on Lori's forearm. It was so touching. It was as if Cassie was saying goodbye to her and letting her know everything would be okay. I thought my heart would shatter.

Lori stood, and with tears in her eyes, hugged me and said, "I'll see you soon."

After she left John and I put Cassie in the back of our SUV. The night before, John had put the back seats down so Cassie could sit between us. I kept looking over at Cassie on the way to the vet clinic. I wanted to take in every last moment with her. She seemed so happy; her tail was swishing back and forth and she almost looked as if she were smiling. I took some small measure in comfort in the fact that she didn't seem to understand where we were going.

Then again, maybe she was happy because she somehow knew that we were helping to end her suffering. I'm certain she knew that we loved her with all our hearts.

When we arrived at the clinic, we were immediately taken to the room where Cassie would be euthanized. Dr. B was on vacation, so Dr. M would administer the shot to ease her into a new world. The technicians took Cassie to the back room to prep her. When they returned, Cassie was laying on a table as they rolled her into the room. Her tail was thumping when she saw us once again. This only added to my heartache of what was about to happen.

Dr. M stood to the side of the table. "Take your time and let me know when you're ready."

"We said our goodbyes last night," I said, crying softly, "We are as ready as we can be."

She nodded, stepped forward and gently administered the shot into Cassie's right fore limb. I held tightly onto Cassie, hugging her around the neck with all my might. I was crying buckets of tears. John stood behind me, petting the top of Cassie's head. It was the hardest thing we ever had to do. I watched her chest rise a few times, and then it became still. I thought the grief of that moment would swallow me whole. Just when I thought I couldn't stand the pain for one moment longer, I looked at Cassie's slightly grayed muzzle and noticed that a peace seemed to wash over her sweet face. Seeing her content and no longer in pain was the only thing that saved me.

I looked up at Dr. M and saw she had tears in her eyes.

I said, "Cassie was such a good dog."

She nodded.

I said, "Thank you."

John and I held hands as we walked out of the clinic without our beloved brown dog. Driving home, I felt like I was in a fog. Everything seemed so surreal. Now and then I would realize we were passing cars and people, out walking or going about their day. It was hard to imagine that I'd ever feel normal again after losing the dog I had wanted so badly and loved so deeply. Just like that, in a blink of an eye, she was gone.

As difficult as the morning had been, John still had to get back to work. When we returned home, he hugged me tightly, then left to check out job sites he needed to attend to. I plopped down in my big red chair, which had always made me feel safe and comforted. All I felt now was incredibly sad and empty. I realized Frankie was at my feet and wanted me to pick her up. I leaned over, scooped her in my arms, and set her on my lap. But not even little Frankie could erase the loss that was heavy in my heart. I held her, but all I really wanted was to hug Cassie once again.

I sat in the chair, staring into the backyard, for what seemed like hours, but when I looked at the clock only a few moments had gone by. I felt as though time would never move again. It was eerily quiet in our house without Cassie, although at one point I could have sworn I heard the click of her toenails across the hardwood floor. I wondered, *did I really hear that, or was it just wishful thinking?*

Suddenly, I didn't want to be home alone. My dad only lives about four blocks from us and I decided to go over there and tell him the news. He was retired and when the weather permitted, he spent most days fishing or golfing. I was happy to find him home. When he answered the door I walked in without even saying hello. "Cassie is gone."

My dad looked at me with a confused expression. "What do you mean, she's gone? Did she run away?"

"No, we put her to sleep this morning," I said, and burst out crying again.

My dad hugged me tight, and having his arms wrapped around me brought some relief from the pain. After a moment, we walked to the living room and sat down on the sofa. We talked about Cassie for a bit, but then I found myself eager to get back to Frankie.

When I returned home, I sat down in my red chair. Frankie had followed me, so I picked her up and put her on my lap. My mom had said she would stop by that afternoon, so I just stared out the living room window and waited for her to arrive.

Around one o'clock, I saw my mom's car pull up, and I walked over to the storm door to let her in. Without a word, she put her arms around me and held me close. I wanted her to take away all the hurt, like she did when I was a little girl. We sat down at the kitchen table and she handed me a small package.

I looked at it and said, "All I want is Cassie back." I burst into tears. I felt like I would never stop crying.

"I know, honey."

I wiped my eyes and opened the package. It was a statue of an angel, hugging a little brown puppy. It was so sweet.

"Thank you, Mom."

She smiled with tears in her eyes.

She listened quietly as I shared the details of Cassie's passing. It was therapeutic to talk about it. I also reminisced about some of my favorite things about Cassie—how I loved to hug her around her soft neck. How I loved to sit quietly and observe her as she sat under the tree in our front yard and watched the world go by. She had always looked so peaceful, and I found this comforting. As I spoke, Mom patted my hand gently, knowing I needed to let it out. After she left I thought about how blessed I was to have a mom who was always here for me, bringing me comfort during difficult times.

A few days later I asked my dad if he would make a wood carving of a heart that said, "Forever Bill's Tree." Bill was one of Cassie's many nicknames. Funny name for a girl dog, I know. But her full name was Cassie Jo, which turned into the nickname Billy Joe, which we eventually shortened to Bill. That name really stuck, and because John and I always said that the maple tree was hers, it seemed fitting to hang a sign in her honor. After my dad delivered the completed heart carving, John nailed it to the maple tree. It became a sweet remembrance of Cassie every time we walked to the mailbox.

In mid-June, a few weeks prior to Cassie's passing, I finished up my coaching with Diane. It was a month earlier than expected, but I felt I had accomplished what I set out to do. Diane also felt I had made significant progress. Even though I was still grieving Cassie, I was finding more joy and purpose in my life.

CHAPTER NINE

New Possibilities

Although there were moments when the tears came unexpectedly, the grief lessened a bit with each passing day. One day, about two weeks after her passing, I actually woke up happy. It felt good to be lighter in my spirit again. I was going about my morning, not really thinking about Cassie—or so I thought. As I was buttering my toast, out of the blue, I burst into tears. As I moved through my days without her, I came to believe in those moments when I thought I heard her toenails on the floor; it was as if Cassie was letting me know she was still with me, just in a different realm. Moments like this were quite comforting for me.

My first article published in the newspaper was a fitting tribute to the big, brown dog with the soulful eyes. Like so many things during that time, it was bittersweet. While, I was proud to see my words in print, I was also struck with fear. As I read it, I thought, *Oh no, now everyone will know how I feel.* It felt a bit vulnerable, but I hoped that by sharing my thoughts on the quality of life for terminally ill pets, I could help others.

As I ran errands in our small town a few days later, I wondered what people thought of the story. Would they think it was strange that I was grieving my pet's passing so deeply? Would they think I had made the wrong decision for her? But I was pleasantly surprised by the number of people who thanked me for sharing my story. What was truly healing, though, was when people said it helped them deal with the loss of their own pet.

While this experience was a big step in my recovery, I wondered how Frankie was doing through all of this. There was no way for me to tell whether she was grieving like I was, however, I did notice that she seemed to be at my side more often than usual. I welcomed the added attention and found comfort in snuggling with her.

The reaction to my article had given me a new awareness of others who had suffered a similar loss. For some reason, I felt particularly compassionate towards those in nursing homes or hospitals; they must miss their pets terribly! I started to consider what it might be like to have a therapy dog, and how that dog could fill a void in other's lives. The dog and I would be a team, and I could write about our experiences at various facilities we visited.

The more I thought about it, the more excited I became. I had always wanted to give back but was never able to figure out what that looked like for me. But this idea really resonated with me. I found myself thinking about the possibilities all the time, and I knew my heart was telling me that this was the answer.

If I did pursue this, I would have to get a new puppy to train as the therapy dog. But first, of course, I would have to discuss it with John. He was still grieving Cassie as well. He enjoyed having a dog at his side each morning and evening as he did chores outside. About two weeks after Cassie's passing, he told me he'd love to have another Lab. I was hesitant at first because the pain was so fresh, but the thought of bringing another puppy home started to warm my heart.

We discussed it, and decided that this time we wanted a yellow Labrador. Once again, I began the diligent search to find a purebred from a good breeder. Cassie had come from what I now realize was a "backyard breeder"—someone who loves the breed, but may not have much experience in breeding. Sadly, there are many who breed animals as a way to bring in a little extra income. They often engage in poor breeding practices that can lead to complications down the line. John and I both wondered whether perhaps Cassie wouldn't have gotten cancer if we had obtained her from a reputable breeder. She had also been diagnosed with severe osteoarthritis at the age of six, and we thought poor breeding may have been a factor there as well.

During the course of my research, I discovered that there are two breeds of Labs. One is the English Labrador, which was first bred in England and is thought to be the original breed. When the breed was discovered in the United States, people fell in love with them and they became overbred, which led to the second breed, the American Labrador. I could clearly see the difference between the English and American Labrador. The English Lab is rather stocky, with a bushy, short tail and boxy head, while the American Lab is usually taller and lankier with a thinner face and head. The American Lab often has a long, thin tail as well. I fell in love with the English Labrador's look and their calm temperament. When I shared this with John, he also fell in love with the English breed.

I was hoping to find a reputable breeder of English Labs in our home state of Wisconsin. The closest one, however, was Greatland Labradors in Tennessee. The moment I saw their website I knew I had found the right breeder. I was impressed that Terri, the owner, only breeds Labradors that are of correct, low-key, easily trainable temperaments, in excellent physical conformation, and display an outstanding desire to retrieve. I also learned that the Labrador is a sporting breed that can be developed as a hunting companion; yet, not all show Labs can hunt and not all hunting Labs can show. Terri also believed that first and foremost, a Labrador should be a great family companion.

I also began to think about a name for our pup. One night we were out in our small town, which is known for its popular race track. It attracts thousands of visitors in the summer months, and this weekend it was hosting vintage car races. Exquisite, older model cars were lined up for the locals and visitors to admire. As we were walking among the crowds of people, I saw a woman sitting off to the side in the grass, petting a big, beautiful German Shepherd. I can never walk by a dog, so I stopped and asked the woman if I could pet the Shepherd. This helped to strike up a conversation.

"Your dog is so beautiful," I said. "What is his or her name?"

"Kylie," the woman replied in a British accent.

As soon as I heard the name roll off the British woman's tongue, I knew without a doubt this was the right name for our little girl. I petted her dog a few moments longer, then thanked the woman for letting me do so.

When I went back to the Greatland website, I was ecstatic to discover that one of their Labs was expecting in late October. I immediately emailed Terri about my interest in getting a pup from her. She wrote back, asking whether we wanted a puppy for family purposes, hunting, or both. I told her I was planning on training my pup to become a therapy dog, as well as a family dog. This information would help her determine which pup would be the best suited for that line of work. I also had to fill out an extensive questionnaire, as she was very particular about where her dogs went. She also had a policy that if after taking the puppy we changed our minds, we had to return the pup to her.

I faxed the completed paperwork to Terri, and it took about a week before I heard back that we had been accepted. I could hardly believe that in the very near future I would be holding a new cuddly puppy in my arms again. I've never really cared to hold newborn babies, but put a puppy in my arms, and it feels like home to me!

We were able to watch the puppies grow via email updates from Terri; and we also regularly checked the website for updated photos. It was an exciting time, but it also seemed to drag out forever as I waited for the day I would smell puppy breath and nurture a little one again. To occupy my mind, I began to study and read about therapy dogs. There are many different organizations that train them, and I carefully read through each website.

I had also been reading books by author Jon Katz. He writes about his life with his dogs, and the book I was reading at the time was *Izzy and Lenore: Two Dogs, an Unexpected Journey, and Me.* Jon's partnership with his dogs as they helped hospice patients fascinated me, especially their experiences with the dying. I was deeply touched by the effect his dogs had with those preparing to leave this world. It was incredibly moving.

The thought of doing this work with my dog both intrigued and frightened me. While I admired Jon's strength in being able to be with someone who is dying, I didn't think I could handle it. Little did I know that someday I would come to appreciate and view the dying in a completely different way. For now, my goal was to get my pup home, trained, and visiting nursing homes and hospitals; this would take a year of hard work.

CHAPTER TEN

Kylie

One day, while on the Greatland website, I noticed that each of the growing pups had a different colored piece of yarn around his or her neck. This was how Terri could tell them apart. About six weeks after the pups were born, Terri shared with me that the pup with the pink yarn necklace was ours. She felt this little one was exhibiting all the characteristics of a good therapy dog: confident, sociable, gentle, polite, calm tempered, and loved to be held. Although I've never had a child, I felt like an expectant mother checking on the growth and progress of my baby pup. Watching her grow and thrive brought me so much joy, and I could hardly wait until I held Kylie in my arms for the first time.

The pups were growing at a rapid pace, and by late fall my little one was all I could think about. We made plans to stay in Nashville, which was not far from the city where the breeder lived.

Three weeks before Christmas, we left town and began the drive to pick up Kylie. I was excited to be getting away on a little vacation, but I was also worried about Frankie. We had left her at the kennel, where she stays whenever we go on vacation; however, this was the first time she would be there without Cassie. Still, I knew she was in good hands. When I dropped Frankie off I shared my concerns with Denise, the kennel's owner and a woman I trusted completely. She completely understood and offered to take Frankie in the house now and then during her stay. This helped to ease my mind, and I was once again looking forward to our adventure.

We arrived in Nashville around dinner time. It would be four days before we would actually meet Kylie. I hoped the sightseeing we had planned would make the days go by fast. We love Tennessee, and had been there several times over the years, staying a day or two before heading to Florida. But now we would get to see more of it, and we even began talking about retiring there someday. It was fun being in Nashville amid the hustle and bustle and sparkling lights of the holiday season. The weather was in the upper 60s, and perfect. We visited to the Grand Ole Opry and many other local attractions during the day; each evening we searched for a good restaurant that had a relaxing atmosphere and a crowded bar so we could people watch. At each meal we talked about meeting Kylie, and how we could hardly wait to see her.

I've always felt so blessed to have a partner that I can talk to. We can talk about almost anything. Some of our best times together have been when we are relaxing and deep in conversation. Talking about our love for Cassie and the new love we'd have for Kylie warmed my heart, and I felt on top of the world. But I couldn't help but think about Frankie too. I called Denise every other day to check in. I was always relieved when she told me Frankie was doing just fine. She would have little stories of Frankie barking at new dogs coming into the kennel, and how happy Frankie was to see her whenever she came out to check on her. She especially liked the special times she got to be in the house with Denise and her husband, and had a nice warm lap to curl up on.

Finally, the day we would meet our new little furry girl arrived. Greatland Breeders was out in the country, and since we weren't sure how long the trip was from Nashville, we set out early, stopping along the way for a quick breakfast. This was our last day in Tennessee; our plan was to pick up Kylie, then head straight back home to Wisconsin.

We arrived in Terri's town at 7 a.m.—two hours ahead of our scheduled appointment. Since we had time to kill, we decided to do a "test run." As we got into the outer area of the city, I was surprised at how many run down homes and properties there were. Many homes had multiple rusty, dilapidated cars in the yard, along with other junk of every sort. But every now and then we'd come across a big, beautiful, brick home with immaculate yards. I started to worry about what we would find at Greatland Labradors, but I didn't voice my concern to John.

We found it a few moments later, as we made our way down the winding road. It was like so many of the rundown homes we had seen along the way, and my heart sank. From the road we could see Terri's mobile home, and off to the side were the dog kennels. From a distance everything looked clean and kept in good condition. This helped put my mind a little more at ease. There was junk scattered in the yard, along with dilapidated cars--definitely not how I would be comfortable living. I found myself feeling a bit guilty for judging on first appearance.

We still had about an hour to kill, so we made note of how long it had taken to arrive there, then we headed out for a bit more sightseeing. We drove in silence for a few moments, then John said, "It's not what I expected."

"I know. I thought the same thing but didn't want to say anything."

"We have to give it a chance since we came all this way."

"I know. And I really want to see Kylie."

"We have to get past any uneasiness we are feeling and not judge the breeder solely on the appearance of her home."

Time seemed to pass slowly as we drove the winding roads. But before we knew it, it was time to turn around and head back to meet Kylie. As we slowly drove into the driveway, the dogs began to bark. All the kennels were full, so it caused quite the commotion. I could see the dogs as we parked at the end of the driveway. They were absolutely beautiful and I found myself wanting to go to each kennel and pet them.

John and I got out of the car and walked up the steps to Terri's home. They were covered in carpeting, which was torn in many places. The front door was open, and the screen door was partially ripped. I rang the doorbell and a moment later, an attractive blonde woman came to the door.

I said, "Hi, my name is Barb and this is my husband, John. We are here to pick up our puppy."

"Terri," she said warmly, holding out a hand. "Please come on in."

We followed her inside and to my surprise, the house was neat and clean. Four kids were scattered around the living room, some on the floor and some on the sofa, watching TV. They didn't look our way. I guess that with their mom's breeding business being operated from their home, they were used to the comings and goings of strangers.

As she motioned for us to sit at the kitchen table, I could hear squealing and yipping coming from another room. After some small talk, Terri said, "I have the puppies in the laundry room if you'd like to follow me."

I nodded enthusiastically. She took us through her kitchen and as we got closer to the pups the squeals got louder. My heart was beating fast in anticipation.

"Here we are," she said.

There was a baby gate across the doorway to keep the pups contained. As I peered in and looked down, I saw all eight wiggly bodies clambering their way to the front of the gate for attention. I was in heaven, seeing all those puppies.

"Which one is ours?" I asked.

Terri bent down and picked up the biggest, fluffiest one of them all. As she put Kylie in my arms, I couldn't control my emotions and tears began rolling down my face.

I was finally holding my new little Lab. She was so plump and soft. My heart was overwhelmed with joy. For just a moment, I also felt a tinge of sadness for the loss of Cassie. Nothing could ever replace her, and I'd always have a special spot in my heart for her, but I also knew I had room to love another dog. I was ready. I had also come to realize with Cassie's passing that for someone like me, who loves animals deeply, to not love another would be such a shame. It is part of who I am. Loving dogs brings me so much happiness. I often think how sad it is when someone is so devastated by the loss of a pet that they can't bring themselves to love another. It's awful to think that person won't feel that joy and love anymore, or give another pet a chance to be loved. But a part of me understands that grief and pain too.

We walked back to the kitchen table and filled out the paperwork, with Kylie nestled in my arms. I thought I was going to burst with joy. I was high as a kite looking at her round, sweet face, her soft brown eyes, and her black button nose. I had hoped she would have a brown nose as I love how that looks on a yellow Lab.

After we had finished the paperwork, Terri asked, "Would you like to meet Kylie's parents?"

I nodded enthusiastically. "Yes, that would be wonderful!"

We walked outside and Terri pointed a few kennels down. "The dog in the third kennel down is Kylie's dad, Justin," she said. He was quite handsome and I was pleased to see how healthy and happy he looked. Terri opened the kennel we were standing in front of and said, "This is Ruby, Kylie's mom."

Ruby was a gorgeous strawberry color. She walked out to greet us with her bushy tail wagging. I bent down to let her sniff Kylie. I felt tears spring to my eyes again. I was feeling bad for taking her little girl from her. But I also knew that this is how things work with animals, and believed that, somehow, Ruby knew it too. As Ruby was sniffing Kylie, I said to her, "Thank you for giving me such a beautiful little girl. I promise I will take good care of her." As if she understood, she licked my cheek. My heart soared.

We thanked Terri, and then it was time for us to begin the long trip home. We had Kylie's small kennel in the back of our SUV. The backseats were folded down and her kennel was placed between the two front passenger seats. That way we'd be able to see her, and she us, the whole way back to Wisconsin.

I had recently read a book that said not to hold a newborn puppy too much because it can cause them to be less self-confident. So having Kylie in her kennel for the ride home seemed like the right thing to do, but it was hard because all I wanted to do was snuggle her close and breathe in her puppy smell. I reminded myself that she was going to be a therapy dog, so creating structure from the beginning seemed like the best bet.

Before we picked Kylie up, Jon and I had both worried that she would cry all the way home. This is common when pups are separated from their litter for the first time. But we were amazed at how well she rode in the car; we didn't hear one peep out of her the entire time. We stopped occasionally to let her out for a potty break. She was good about sniffing out a spot and doing her duty. I must have looked back at Kylie at least one hundred times to admire her during the trip. Each time I did, I would feel my heart ooze with love for such a beautiful little being. Once, I took a peek and saw that she was sleeping contently. Even though I have never felt like I had a motherly instinct, my eyes filled with tears when I saw that my sweet little girl was happy.

It was nighttime when we finally arrived home. As I always feel when I am away from my dogs, I wished I could run right to the kennel where Frankie was staying and bring her home. I missed her so much. But that would have to wait until morning.

I didn't know how Kylie might do being in a strange new place. We had a kennel set up in our kitchen, where she would stay during the night. I planned to kennel train her so in the future she would look at her kennel as her safe place to go when we were gone. I had never done that with Cassie and wished I had. That first night, I hugged Kylie tight and told her I loved her, then I placed her in the kennel. I didn't hear a whimper out of her until around 2 a.m. I took her outside to go potty, then it was back to her kennel. She went without a fuss and slept straight through until 7 a.m.

After feeding Kylie her breakfast, I played with her for awhile. I hugged her goodbye, letting her know I'd be back soon with her sister, Frankie.

I was anxious to pick up Frankie and introduce her to her new dog sister. Before we had left for Tennessee, I told Frankie all about Kylie and that she would soon have a new companion to play with. She wagged her tail as I talked, but whether she understood or not, I didn't have a clue. But I knew she loved to play and cuddle with Cassie so I felt confident she would take to Kylie in no time at all.

When I arrived at the kennel, Frankie was out in the fenced-in area by herself, which was quite comical to see. It was such a big yard for a little short dog. She looked so darling and it made me smile. As I got out of my car I walked toward her and she started wagging her tail. I swear if I had clocked it, it was going over one hundred miles a minute. I've always loved dachshund's tails, as there is no denying how happy they are to see you.

I said, in my high squeaky voice, "Hi, my little sweet pea! How are you? I missed you soooo much!"

Denise walked down from the house, smiling, and said, "Frankie was a very good girl." Although she probably tells all pet parents that, even if their pets are wild beasts, I took it all in as if my little one was the best dog in the world.

I was anxious to get back home so Frankie and Kylie could meet. I quickly paid Denise, thanked her, and headed to my car with Frankie prancing happily beside me on her leash. Frankie always sat on my lap, with the front part of her body over my arm, so she could place her front paws on the top part of the car door and look out the window. I couldn't stop kissing the top of her soft head and giving her little squeezes all the way home. Having her in my arms made me feel complete.

When I got back home I picked up Frankie and held her in my arms. I wanted to introduce the dogs slowly. I bent down so they could sniff each other. As I did, both their tails began to wag. This was a good sign, so I put Frankie on the floor next to Kylie. They took to each other as if they had always been best pals. They checked each other out, followed each other around, and even roughhoused a little bit.

It always amazes me how dogs seem to accept other animals and humans without judgment. It wasn't long before the two were cuddled up together on Frankie's large pink pillow, sound asleep. Looking at them happy and content, I felt my heart soar once again. The void of losing Cassie would always be with me, and I would continue to miss her, but Kylie filled that place in me that needed to love another dog. My family was once again complete.

CHAPTER ELEVEN

Puppy Antics

Christmas was a little over a week away and I was in a truly happy place in my life. John's business was going well, my writing was bringing me great joy, and I was excited that January would soon be here. It meant that I would be taking Kylie to her first puppy training class. After that, I planned to enroll her in obedience training so that when she turned one year old, I could have her tested to become a therapy dog. John and I were also busy planning a vacation to Florida in April. Life was good.

Puppy training classes were a new experience for me and I enjoyed watching Kylie learn new things. During the first few classes though, I was concerned because Kylie would cower under my chair before each class began. She was shy with some of the dogs. But one golden retriever named Lady, who had lots of energy, a short attention span, and a bit of a naughty streak, always coaxed Kylie out to play.

Each week Kylie and I looked forward to class. She always rode happily in the back of my car, seats folded down, and in her wire kennel so she had a good view. Then she would prance right into the training center. She was still shy when she first saw the other dogs, and it took her some time before her tail came from between her legs.

She caught on easily to the commands of sit, stay, heel, and down, and I felt immensely proud. My heart would melt whenever I looked at her little round face and big brown eyes as she watched me for her next instruction. I felt a deep bond forming between the two of us. I loved how we were becoming a team.

At home, Kylie and Frankie continued to do well together, and though Kylie could be kind of rough sometimes, I knew it was just the puppy in her. Soon I was able to leave them together alone in the kitchen for short amounts of time, while I worked in our home office.

One day they were quiet as could be, having settled in after I fed them lunch. I assumed they were sleeping. When an hour went by and I hadn't heard them stir, I went to check on them. As I walked into the kitchen, I discovered Kylie had chewed up one of the area rugs near our front door. I looked at her, frustrated, and mildly scolded her. I had caught her chewing the rug once before, but I knew I couldn't really yell at her, because the damage was done and she wouldn't know why I was reprimanding her. I cleaned up the tattered rug and bits of carpet fibers, throwing everything in the trash, and then headed back to my office.

Later that afternoon, Frankie threw up. It seemed like an awful lot for such a small dog. I was concerned, but tried not to worry. Maybe something just didn't agree with her, I thought. I checked on her often, and she seemed fine the rest of the day. She ate dinner and later that night off to bed we went. Frankie always slept with us, and that night she snuggled in next to John and slept through until morning.

In the morning I fed the girls their breakfast and about an hour later, Frankie threw up again, and again, it was a large amount. Now I was really concerned, so I called the vet's office. I told the receptionist about Frankie vomiting that morning, and once the day before. She transferred me to a veterinarian technician. The technician asked me if I knew if Frankie had gotten into anything.

"Was she outside? Could she have gotten into some antifreeze?"

"No, because we know how dangerous it is, so we and don't have it sitting around."

"Do you notice any of her toys missing? Sometimes they will eat a toy and it gets lodged in their stomach."

I did a quick scan around the kitchen, living room, and bedroom.

"No, there aren't any toys missing and they are all in one piece."

"Have you given her any new treats?"

"Nope, no new treats either."

"I'll need to consult with a vet and one of us will get back to you soon."

"Okay, thank you."

A few minutes later she called me back and said, "Dr. Q said if you're sure she didn't get into anything and you haven't given her any new food or treats, there's probably no cause for concern, unless of course she continues to throw up. For now, feed her a bland diet of boiled chicken and rice and keep an eye on her. Let us know how that goes."

"Okay, I'll do that."

I took a chicken breast out of the freezer and scurried off to the grocery store to buy some rice for her dinner that evening.

When I returned home I couldn't find Frankie anywhere. I kept calling her, but she didn't come, which was unusual. Finally, I looked under the bed as she likes to go under it once in a while. I was relieved to find her there, but realized she was throwing up again. As I was reaching to pull her out from under the bed, I noticed four huge areas of dried vomit on the rug.

I cried out, "Oh, my gosh, Frankie, what's wrong?"

My heart racing with fear, I picked her up and immediately called the vet's office. When I told them what I had found they told me to bring her in immediately.

I rushed her to the clinic, which is about ten minutes from our home, praying the whole way that she would be alright. As soon as I arrived, they took us back to an exam room where the vet technician and Dr. Q asked me the same questions again about missing toys, a new treat I may have fed her, et cetera. Again, I said no to all the questions. Then I remembered that Kylie had torn up the carpet the morning before.

"Do you think Frankie could have eaten part of the rug?" I asked.

"It is quite possible, but the only way to know is to do an x-ray. We will need to sedate her and if we see a blockage we'll need to go in right away."

I told them okay, that they should do whatever was necessary.

"It will take time to do the x-ray," Dr. Q explained. "It would be best for you to go home and wait for us to call with the results."

I drove home, praying out loud all the way, begging God to please let

Frankie be okay. The thought that I might lose her, especially so soon after Cassie's death, was unbearable.

When I got home, I tried to work but I just couldn't concentrate. I just sat there and stared out the window and continued to pray. An hour later, the phone rang. It was Dr. Q.

"We did the x-ray and there appears to be something suspicious in Frankie's intestine. We need to go in right away and do surgery."

"Oh, my gosh. Is she going to be okay?"

"I think we caught this in time. I'll call you as soon as I am out of surgery."

When I got off the phone I called John to let him know what was happening. As I always do when I have a crisis with my pets, I also called my sister-in-law Lori and my mom and asked them to pray for Frankie.

Another hour passed before I heard the phone ring again. I quickly said out loud as I reached for the phone, "Please let Frankie be okay." It was Dr. Q again.

"Frankie is out of surgery and is doing well. But we found carpet fiber in her intestine. Actually, part of the fiber was wound *around* her intestine. If you waited another hour to bring her in, she may not have made it. You likely just saved her life."

My heart just about beat out of my chest when he told me the news. Holding in the tears, I said, "Wow! I can't believe it. Thank you for everything."

"You are welcome. She should be okay to go home in the morning."

As I hung up the phone it really hit home that I had almost lost my little girl. I broke down and cried. After a few moments I pulled myself together. I knew I needed to call John, my mom and Lori to let them know Frankie was going to be fine. Their prayers certainly helped, and I was grateful.

The next morning I went to the clinic to bring Frankie home. She was still a bit out of it, but recovered beautifully over the next few days. I was also able to continue training classes with Kylie without any interruption. Kylie passed the training with flying colors and graduated from obedience classes. I was so proud. Our next step was to take the advanced obedience training. But before we would do that, John and I had plans to drive to Florida for a much needed vacation.

John's business had been thriving, which made trying to get away difficult. While Cassie had cancer it was also important to me to be with her until she passed. Going on vacation was out of the question then. I would never have forgiven myself if Cassie had died while we were away. Now we felt the time was right to finally get some rest and relaxation. It felt good to pack up the car and know we would soak up some sun and fun for ten days.

The afternoon before we left, I took Kylie and Frankie to the kennel. Frankie knew the kennel well, but this time I was concerned about Kylie. She was only six months old and had never been away from us. I hoped she would adjust. My original plan was to have Kylie stay in the same kennel with Frankie so they could keep each other company, just like when Cassie and Frankie stayed together. But the more I thought about it, I decided that it would be better if they each had their own kennel.

When I arrived, I asked Denise if it would be possible for Kylie and Frankie to be in separate but adjacent kennels that way they could at least see each other. I explained that Kylie, still being a young pup with tons of energy, didn't always realize her own strength. I didn't want her to play too rough with Frankie. In the absence of twenty –four hour supervision, I felt this was the best for both of them. She understood and happily accommodated my request.

I felt like a nervous nelly leaving Kylie for the first time. I didn't want her to be lonely or think I had deserted her. Denise brought us to the back part of the facility so I could put the girls in their kennels and say goodbye.

I put Frankie in her kennel first, along with her large pink pillow so she would have a nice soft spot to lie on. Then I placed Kylie in her kennel, but didn't have a pillow for her. I feared she may chew it up and I didn't want to take the chance.

Pointing to Frankie, I said to Kylie, "See, your sister is right next door, so you can see her."

I put their food, leashes, and extra blankets in the large plastic containers that were kept in each kennel. Then I hugged Frankie and then Kylie and tried not to cry as I closed each door to their kennels. I would miss them so much. But I silently reminded myself that they were in good hands with Denise. I quickly walked away without looking back and headed to my car.

Once I was back home, I began to focus on our vacation. This helped take my attention away from missing my dogs.

CHAPTER TWELVE

The Call

We were up early the next morning and on the road by 5 a.m. We planned to drive to Tennessee the first day and stay for two days before making our final leg of the trip to Florida. My mom and her husband, David, have a second home in Englewood, Florida; so, besides being on vacation, I was also excited about seeing my mom.

We did some sightseeing while in Tennessee. It felt good to chill out and relax. It had been so long since our last vacation, and in that time we had dealt with so many stressful things. Finally, we had the chance to think about nothing but relaxing.

It was the day before Easter when we arrived in Florida, and late afternoon by the time we reached my mom's development. As we wound our way through the gated community, my anticipation about seeing my mom grew. A few moments later we pulled up in front of the house, and she and David walked out the front door to greet us. Before our car even came to a stop, I jumped out and ran to hug her.

After leaving my full time job years earlier, I was able to spend more time with my mom. Naturally, we grew much closer. Whether went out to lunch, shopping, or just hanging out together at her house or mine, I treasured each moment with her. I was excited about doing all those things once again now that we had finally arrived.

John and I took some luggage out of the car and Mom showed us to the bedroom where we would be staying. It looked out over the lanai with a beautiful pool. I felt like I was in heaven.

That evening we went to dinner at a casual restaurant right on the ocean, and got a table outside. We ordered a round of cocktails and talked about our time in Tennessee. Hearing the ocean, and being with my mom, David, and John, I felt myself melt into complete relaxation mode.

On Easter Sunday we woke up to bright sunshine streaming through the bedroom windows and a tropical breeze blowing through the open patio door. I smiled as I looked at John. My mom made us breakfast and we talked about what we would do for the day. John and I decided we would love to walk along the ocean, so after visiting with my mom and David for a while, we hopped in the car for some time to ourselves.

It felt odd but wonderful to be walking barefoot along the ocean on Easter. If we were home we'd likely be with John's family, having a traditional Easter brunch.

After enjoying the sights and sounds of the ocean, we found a nearby restaurant for lunch. Sitting outside under a big umbrella on a faded deck, I ordered a margarita on the rocks and John ordered a beer. There was a band playing under the tiki hut and people were dressed in shorts and tank tops, or swimsuits. We soaked in each glorious moment of the sun and the laid back atmosphere.

A few hours later we headed back to my mom's, where I went for a swim in the pool. We decided to stay in for the evening and have steak and lobster my mom had taken out of the freezer. I was looking forward to more conversation and a delicious meal.

We had all just settled into our chairs along the kitchen island, enjoying a cocktail, when the phone rang. My mom picked up the phone. A moment later I heard her say, "Sure just a minute."

As she handed me the phone she said, "It's Lori."

"Hi, Lori," I said.

"I'm sorry to be calling around the dinner hour but I'm with Frankie at the clinic with Dr. Q. Frankie is seriously hurt."

I didn't quite understand what she was talking about. "What do you mean?"

"I'm going to put Dr. Q on the line and he will explain."

"Hi, Barb, it's Dr. Q. Yes, Frankie appears to have ruptured a disk in her back. She doesn't have any deep pain sensation. The rupture has caused paralysis in her hind legs. Time is of the essence if she is to recover and walk again. She has to go to the Animal Referral Center for surgery, right away. I just need your permission to let Lori take Frankie there, then I'll call to let them know they are on their way."

"Okay, but how did this happen?"

"Well, from what Lori has told me, it seems that when Denise went to check on Frankie she noticed the large plastic container in the kennel was tipped over. Frankie was sitting beside it. We *think* Frankie may have tried to jump up onto the container and it tipped over, causing Frankie to fall on the cement. This could have been what caused the disc to rupture."

My head spinning, I asked, "Is Frankie in any pain?"

"No, she isn't in any pain."

"Where is the Animal Referral Center?"

"It's located in Appleton."

I was in total shock and was trying to hold back my tears. "What does this mean? What will they do in Appleton?"

"They will confirm if Frankie indeed does have a ruptured disk. If she does, they will need to do surgery as soon as possible."

"What is the cost of the surgery?"

"I'm not sure of an exact cost, but I believe it is somewhere between $3,000 and $5,000."

My heart fell to my feet. We didn't have that kind of money, but I knew my little girl needed help.

I began to cry. "Yes, please have Lori take Frankie to the Animal Referral Center."

"I'll call them then to advise the clinic that Frankie is on the way. Here's Lori again."

By then I was sobbing.

Lori said, "Don't worry. I'll take good care of Frankie for you." I knew she would, but I felt incredibly helpless, so many miles away. I wanted to be with Frankie and hold her, and tell her everything would be okay. I couldn't say anything because I was crying so hard. "I'll call you when we get there."

I managed to say, "Okay, thank you," before hanging up the phone.

I remember standing at the corner of the kitchen island, bent over as if I was going to pass out, and crying hysterically. My poor family didn't know the whole story yet. It took several tries for me to get the words out and let them know what was happening.

After explaining everything, I said, "What if Frankie doesn't walk again?" I just couldn't picture what this would mean for her life.

"And," I added, "Dr. Q said the surgery will cost anywhere from $3,000 to $5,000. We don't have that kind of money just lying around."

Nothing was confirmed yet, and my mom tried to remain optimistic. "Don't worry about the money right now. We will help you if need be. Maybe Frankie won't need surgery. We won't know until Lori gets her to the clinic."

This helped calm me down. She was right. We didn't know all the facts. We would need to wait. I held out hope that everything would turn out okay. I tried my best to stay positive. Dinner was ready, though I found it hard to eat. I was trying to calm down, but I just wanted to know the outcome. It was difficult waiting to hear back from Lori.

We had just finished up dinner when the phone rang again. It was Lori calling from the Animal Referral Clinic.

"The vet just took Frankie back to the exam room. She will call you shortly."

"How is Frankie doing?"

"Other than her little legs not working, she is doing very well."

"Oh, that makes me feel a little better. Thank you."

"I took Frankie's pink pillow from the kennel and she laid on it next to me on the ride here." It comforted me to picture her snuggled on her pillow. To lighten the mood a bit, Lori said, "I have a cute little story."

"You do? What is it?"

"I wrapped Frankie in a blanket before I brought her into the clinic. I was holding her and all of a sudden I smelled something. I looked down and saw poop on the floor. I looked to an older couple in the waiting area and said, "Did Frankie do that?' They smiled and nodded their heads."

I chuckled.

Lori said, "I didn't realize her little butt was hanging out the end of the blanket."

I laughed at the scene she described and before hanging up again, thanked her once again for being there for Frankie.

A few moments later the phone rang again. The vet on call that evening introduced herself as Dr. C. She said, "I just finished examining Frankie. I'm quite sure she has a ruptured disc in her back. To confirm this, we will need to do a myelogram. I'll need your permission to do this procedure."

Never having heard of this procedure I said, "What is a myelogram?"

She explained they needed to inject a special dye into the space between the membranes that surround Frankie's spinal cord. If there was a herniated or severely bulging disc, it would block the dye's progress. She said it would take about a half hour to complete.

"Okay, please go ahead."

When the second call came from Dr. C, she confirmed that Frankie's disc was ruptured. She would need surgery as soon as possible. Since I had held out hope that this wasn't going to be the case, I was devastated by the news.

She explained, "From what I can tell with the rupture and given the time that has passed since we think it ruptured, she has about a ten percent chance of walking again. But I'd like the surgeon to confirm my diagnosis. Would you like the surgeon to call you after she examines Frankie?"

My voice shaking with fear and confusion, I said, "Yes."

As I hung up the phone, I sat there in disbelief. I couldn't believe that Frankie only had a ten percent chance of walking again, even with surgery. How could this be? What was I going to do? I also worried I may never see Frankie alive again whether I opted for the surgery or not. There is always a risk with any surgery and thinking back to her emergency surgery less than two months ago, I worried if she could take another one. More than anything, I was scared if I didn't opt for the surgery that I'd eventually have to put her to sleep. I didn't know much about back problems typical in Dachshunds. When I got Frankie as a pup I knew that they could have back issues, but I had no idea what that truly meant. Now here it was, staring me in the face. I was scared to death that I was going to lose Frankie.

It didn't take long before the phone rang again, and this time it was the surgeon. She explained that after examination and looking at the myelogram, she felt that Frankie had about a ten to thirty percent chance of complete recovery. But she also said there were no guarantees that the surgery would be a success.

My head was spinning and I felt sick to my stomach. "What if Frankie doesn't walk again? What will her quality of life be like? How will she get around? Will she be in pain?" I had so many questions!

The surgeon's voice was very soothing. "I absolutely understand all your concerns. If Frankie doesn't walk again, she can be fitted for a dog cart. These little dogs do remarkably well with them."

I had never heard of such a thing. "What do you mean by a dog cart?"

"They are like wheelchairs, similar to ones used for people, but these are wheelchairs made for dogs like Frankie, who have back issues. Many dogs adjust and go on to live, full, long, happy lives."

I just didn't know what to do. I wanted so badly for Frankie to be okay. I wanted to wake up and realize this was just a bad dream. But it wasn't, and I needed to make a very difficult decision. "I need to talk this over with my husband and call you back."

"I understand. But just remember time is of the essence. If you opt for the surgery, we really need to do it soon."

I hung up the phone, crying and shaking. I was at such a loss of what to do. I had so many emotions and feelings running through me. John and I talked briefly in the bedroom.

Because Frankie was my dog, and John wasn't sure what to do either, he said, "You do what you feel is best. I'll support whatever you decide."

My mom was in her bedroom reading, so I walked through the living room and called outside her bedroom door, "Mom? Can I talk to you?"

"Sure, honey. I'll be right there."

We sat on the couch and I voiced every concern I had to her. "What if the surgery doesn't work and Frankie is permanently paralyzed?" Still not sure about the wheelchair, I said, "Will she truly be happy not having the use of her back legs?" I just couldn't picture her not being able to walk. I pictured this pitiful sight and wondered if she would adjust to a wheelchair. *What if she didn't even make it through surgery?* I couldn't bear the thought of never seeing her alive again. As hard as it is for me to write this, the reality was that I questioned if I could take care of a handicapped dog. Even harder to admit is the fact that I didn't know whether I wanted the responsibility. As those thoughts ran through my head, I got angry.

"This isn't fair, Mom," I cried, "I had my whole life planned out. I want Kylie to be my therapy dog. Now I will have to put that all on hold to take care of Frankie. I don't understand why God is doing this to me? I just lost Cassie, and now this? Why me? I love animals so much."

Quietly she said, "God only gives you what you can handle."

"Well He is wrong this time. I can't handle this!" The truth is, looking back, I didn't *want* to handle this. I wanted what I had planned for my life. I didn't want to have to deal with this. I worked so hard with my coach, digging deep into my soul to discover what I wanted, and I thought I had figured it all out. I was happy and fulfilled, so how could this be happening? When I look back on those moments, I see the wisdom of my mom come shining through, but at the time I couldn't. "I just don't understand, Mom. I want Kylie to be my therapy dog and now I might not be able to do that."

"Well, maybe God meant for *Frankie* to be your therapy dog."

For as long as I live, I'll never ever forget my mom saying that. Even though I had no idea what it really meant, something in that statement made my heart stir, though I couldn't really explain why at the time. But I knew then, without a doubt, that I had to give Frankie a chance.

CHAPTER THIRTEEN

Devastating Diagnosis

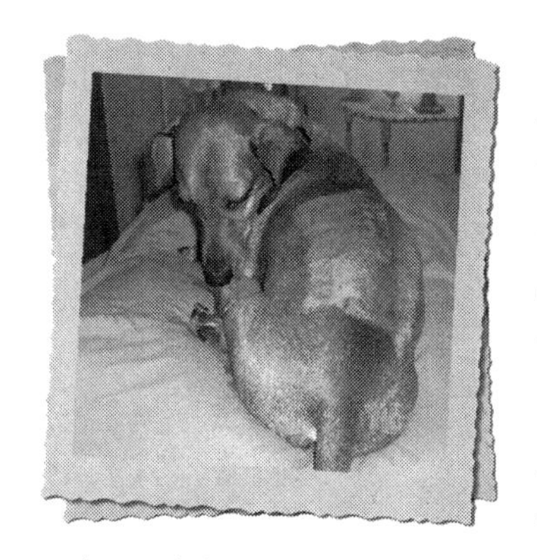

Frankie went into surgery at midnight. An hour later, the surgeon called to report that the surgery went well and Frankie was resting comfortably. Before we hung up she said, "Time will tell whether or not Frankie will walk again."

I was relieved to know that Frankie had made it through the surgery. But then I worried about her recovery and getting home to be with her as soon as possible. John and I were lying in bed after the call.

"I have to get home to be near Frankie. There is no way I can enjoy vacation now."

"I know," he said. "I can't either. We will leave first thing in the morning."

I tried to sleep, but so many thoughts were running through my head that I couldn't relax. John didn't sleep either.

By morning, I was exhausted but eager to get going. I didn't have much of an appetite, either, but I managed to eat a piece of peanut butter toast before hugging my mom goodbye and walking out to the car.

We were on the road by 8 a.m. and it felt good to know I was doing *something* by heading home.

Later that morning as John was driving down the highway, I called the clinic to check on Frankie. I talked with one of the veterinarian technicians.

"Frankie is doing well. She seems happy and alert."

"We are on the road and headed back home. It will take us two days."

"Frankie needs to be here for another two days, so that is perfect timing."

The technician went over the home nursing care I would need to do for Frankie.

"Frankie has a pain patch on, plus she is on Prednisone. She will eventually need to be weaned off the Prednisone. The pain patch will come off in seven days. You'll also need to confine her to a crate for six to eight weeks. She will only be allowed out for potty breaks."

"Why does she need to be confined in a crate?"

"Because this is a spinal injury, we want her to remain as immobile as possible to give her back a chance to heal and recover."

"What about when I have to feed her?"

"You'll need to feed her in her crate also. Strict rest is essential to give her the best possible chance of recovering."

"Okay, I understand."

"When you pick Frankie up Wednesday morning, a technician on duty will show you how to express Frankie's bladder and bowels."

"What do you mean?"

"Because of the paralysis, Frankie doesn't have control of her bodily functions."

"Oh no, I'm not sure I'll be able to learn that."

"Don't worry; it's not that hard to do. The fact that she's a female makes it a bit easier. Males are harder to express. I've expressed her a few times today and she is quite easy to do."

Not exactly convinced, I said, "Oh . . . okay."

As I hung up the phone I started to worry about how I was going to adjust my schedule to help Frankie. New questions ran through my mind. *Will I be able to do this? How would I know when she had to go to the bathroom? Would I have to do this the rest of her life?* Luckily I worked from home, so that eased my mind somewhat. Even though I worried about all the unknowns, I just wanted to see Frankie again.

I had a lot of time to think as we drove. In fact, think was *all* I did! Frankie didn't have the use of her back legs. *How did her back end look?* I wondered. I didn't want to ask the technician because I felt embarrassed. I wondered if she would she think it superficial of me to ask.

Later that afternoon I called Lori to thank her again for all she had done for Frankie, and to give her an update on Frankie's condition. As we talked, I decided to express my concern to her and said, "What does Frankie look like? I mean, with her back legs paralyzed?"

"Well, you know how we always say Frankie looks like a little seal when she sits and her front paws point out to the sides?"

"Yes."

"Well, picture her back end sort of looking like a seal too."

I could cry as I write that sentence right now. One, because it brings up so much anxiety around everything I was feeling in what had transpired in those twenty-four hours after learning about Frankie's back injury. But most of all, because I felt it was the most thoughtful and kind thing anyone could have said to me. It helped put the sweetest image in my mind and helped me feel a little more at ease while I waited to see Frankie again.

The next two days were among the longest of my life. After driving for about twelve hours the first day, we stopped at a hotel for the night. The next day we arrived back in our small town; it was late Tuesday afternoon. We were both exhausted and couldn't wait to sleep in our own bed. Before we had left on vacation, I had washed and hung our bedding out on the line and laying there in the fresh, clean sheets helped make me feel a little less anxious.

We quickly unpacked the car. I then headed out once again to pick Kylie up from the kennel. When I arrived, Denise was waiting for me. I had called her earlier that day letting her know what time I'd be stopping by. The minute she saw me she began to cry. I started to cry too and we hugged.

She said, "I feel so responsible for what happened to Frankie."

"I absolutely don't blame you, Denise. This wasn't your fault."

I did my best to assure her I didn't blame her in any way whatsoever. But she had a hard time dealing with the fact that Frankie was hurt while under her care. I can only imagine, as I know I would feel the same way. People have asked me if had any anger towards Denise, and I always tell them, absolutely not. It would be a waste of time to put the blame on her for so many reasons, but most of all because she truly was not at fault.

"What is Frankie's prognosis?"

"We don't really know yet. Time will tell. But I was told if Frankie is to walk again we should see some signs within the next few weeks."

"I talked to my husband, and we don't know how much the surgery was, but we'd like to pay for it."

"No, Denise, I would never expect that. Frankie is my responsibility."

She truly felt terrible for what happened and wanted to help in some way. But again, I tried my best to reassure her that I didn't hold her accountable. I meant that with all my heart. Even though I was struggling with the unknown and wondering if Frankie would walk again, I knew I had to move forward. I wanted Denise to also. If there is one thing I could change, I wish Frankie's rupture hadn't happened at Denise's kennel. I have never blamed her or held her at fault. As I would learn more about back issues in Dachshunds in the next coming days, I came to discover that this is a disease common in the breed. It is called Intervertebral Disc Disease (IVDD). The theory is that because Dachshunds backs are so long it puts pressure on their spines. Over time the discs in their spine can degenerate, and this can cause a ruptured disc. There is no definite cause, but many theories.

We finally walked back to the area of the kennel where Kylie was staying. I was anxious to see her. Denise and I both smiled for the first time as we rounded the corner and saw Kylie. Kylie's tail began to wag like crazy when she saw us.

"Hey baby girl, I missed you!"

As I opened the gate to the kennel, I bent down and Kylie wiggled her butt right up against me, her tail slapping wildly against my leg. She couldn't get close enough to me. It felt so good to hug her.

Denise walked us to our car and I hugged her again. "Please keep me posted on how Frankie is doing."

"I absolutely will."

It felt good to have Kylie home again. And as I climbed into bed that night those clean, sweet-smelling sheets felt like a warm, safe hug. Still, I was anxious about the next morning when I would see Frankie. When I had talked with Lori the day before, she offered to drive me to the Animal Referral Clinic. I knew I would be a basket-case, so I was relieved to not have to worry about driving.

The next morning, Lori arrived around 9 a.m. I had placed Frankie's kennel out on the sidewalk in front of the house so we could leave the minute she arrived. As she pulled into the driveway, I was out the door, eager to get going. When we saw each other, we hugged, and I started to cry. "I can't thank you enough for all you have done for Frankie."

"You are very welcome."

We hopped in the car and headed north. The clinic was about an hour drive from my home. I don't recall much of the conversation because all I could think about was holding Frankie in my arms once again.

An hour later we pulled into the clinic parking lot. I felt big knots of stress in my stomach. Even though I couldn't wait to see Frankie, I also was scared, wondering how she would look. I took a few deep breaths and remembered what Lori had told me about Frankie looking like a seal. That calmed me a little.

As we walked through the front doors of the clinic, my legs felt like wet noodles. I approached the front desk and told the receptionist my name, and that I was here to pick up Frankie. The young woman looked confused as she flipped through her charts, and I began to think something bad had happened. But a moment later a vet technician was walking by and overheard the confusion. She said, "I'm taking care of Frankie. I just checked on her and she is alert and happy."

I placed my hand on my heart and heaved a big sigh of relief.

"I'll let the surgeon know you're here."

"Thank you."

Lori and I sat down, but not for very long. Five minutes later a vet tech asked us to follow her to the exam room. As we walked down the hallway, I felt butterflies in my stomach. Lori and I took a seat in the exam room. The technician explained that the surgeon who had done Frankie's surgery wasn't in today, but another surgeon who has done this type of surgery before, Dr. H, would be meeting with us. A few moments later he came into the room.

I stood up and shook his hand. "Hi, I'm Frankie's mom, Barb."

"Nice to meet you."

He was rather good looking, which actually helped ease some of my stress. He explained that Frankie's rupture had occurred in the Thoracolumbar, T 12, 13. "That area is actually about three inches from the base of where Frankie's tail starts," he told us. "That is a common area where ruptures can occur in the Dachshund breed. As far as her prognosis, we aren't one hundred percent sure when the rupture occurred. Given the time that elapsed before she had the surgery, I can't be sure of her outcome."

This brought tears to my eyes. I felt so guilty, for her injury. "Could I have done something to prevent this?"

He shook his head. "Not likely. This is a common disease in the breed. Because of their long spines, their discs can degenerate over time, and then at some point there is a possibility of a rupture. Keeping them off furniture, and limited use of stairs, as well as keeping their weight under control is important. But to be honest with you, I've seen Dachshunds that are crazy, who run around the yard wildly and fly off furniture and nothing ever happens to them. And then I've had Dachshunds who don't do any of this and have the condition. Some are just more prone to the disease."

I thought about her activities. She always stayed on the bed when we were gone, but when we returned, she'd fly off the end of the bed to greet us. John had built little stairs that she used to climb onto the bed, but she never used them coming down. I also felt guilty for the first few years of her life when she was overweight. For a time she weighed twenty pounds, which was too much for her frame.

I wanted with all my heart to believe Frankie would walk again, but I knew there was a chance she wouldn't. I needed to know all the facts, so I forced myself to ask about the dog carts even though I was afraid it would "jinx" Frankie's recovery.

"Just in case Frankie doesn't walk again, can you tell me about dog carts?"

"I don't personally know much about the dog carts, but I'm sure their website will answer your questions." He handed me a brochure of a company he recommended.

I took the brochure and tucked it in my purse.

"The technician will get Frankie now, if you're ready.

"Yes! I am ready."

"She will show you how to express Frankie's bladder, as well as go over all the home care Frankie will need."

I extended my hand to shake his hand again. "Thank you so much."

"You're welcome. Good luck with everything."

A few moments later the technician walked in with Frankie nestled in her arms. I immediately got choked up and my eyes misted over with tears. All my fears of how she would look vanished. "Oh, Frankie!" I exclaimed, "I'm so happy to see you!"

I carefully took her from the technician's arms. Frankie was wiggling back and forth, licking my face. I knew this meant she was happy to see me. It took a few moments for Frankie to settle down. Once she did, I was able to see she had lost some weight. Her legs just hung down in the back and looked rather skinny. It was hard to see her in his condition. I also realized that because of the paralysis, her tail didn't wag. That was one of the hardest things for me to accept. To see it lying so still, with no life, made me feel incredibly sad.

I quickly turned my attention back to the technician when she said, "I'd like to show you how to express Frankie's bladder."

"Ok." I was so nervous, but knew I needed to learn how to do this.

The technician placed Frankie's front legs on the exam table and held her back end up, with her hands slightly below Frankie's stomach. "You will need to feel for Frankie's bladder which is just below her waist."

I watched where she placed her hands.

"When Frankie's bladder is full, it will feel sort of like a balloon full of water."

I nodded.

"All you have to do is squeeze gently on either side of her bladder to empty it." As she did this, nothing came out. "Frankie just urinated about an hour before you arrived, so her bladder is likely empty."

"What if I can't express her bladder?"

"It will take some practice, but try not to worry. Frankie is quite easy to express. If you don't get to her in time the urine will leak out, but it's important to still express her after that so all the urine is extracted. If you don't, she could get a bladder infection."

I gave it a try and felt for what I thought was her bladder. It felt awkward and I wasn't sure I was doing it right. And since she didn't have to go, it made it a bit trickier to know if I was squeezing in just the right area. Though I was nervous and apprehensive, I was determined to learn how to help her go to the bathroom. I knew if I had complications I could always visit my local veterinarian's office, so I tried not to worry too much.

"Well what about her bowels? Does she have any control over those?"

"No. That is a muscle. When she has a bowel movement it will just come out on its own." The thought of that didn't make me too happy. She said, "It will take some getting used to, but over time you will figure out a schedule and know when she has to go." I wasn't so sure I would get the hang of it. "Typically, she will have to urinate every one to three hours after she eats or drinks water. You may want to restrict her water to only when she eats so you can pinpoint better when she will have to go. To help her with a bowel movement, you can stimulate her anal glands with a Q-tip or massage around her anal glands."

With the major home care instructions out of the way, she explained the pain patch would need to be removed in seven days. She also explained the medication Frankie was on and how I would need to wean her off it over the next eight weeks. It was a lot to remember and I was feeling quite stressed and hoping I would do everything right.

After paying the bill, which I put on my credit card knowing my mom would be helping me make payments, we headed to Lori's car for the drive home. Lori still had Frankie's large pink pillow in the car. I handed Frankie to Lori and got in the passenger side of the car. I placed the pillow on my lap and Lori gently placed Frankie on the pillow.

Lori needed to stop at a grocery store on our way home, so I stayed in the car with Frankie. As I sat there waiting, I couldn't stop looking at Frankie. I was so thankful to be holding her again. As I gazed down at her, tears started to roll down my cheeks. "I'll do whatever I can to help you walk again, Frankie."

Her sweet brown fawn eyes looked up at me as if to say, "It's okay, Mom. I know you will."

I hugged her, but was afraid to squeeze her too tight because of her back injury. She also looked frail. But in that moment, I had no doubt we had just connected on a deeper level.

We finally arrived home, and I thanked Lori once again for being there for us.

I got her settled in the small crate I had brought her home in as a pup. She settled into her blankets and soon was fast asleep. She slept a lot because of the pain patch and other medication she was on. Later that day, I tried expressing her bladder for the first time and was relieved when it went well. I didn't worry too much at this point about her bowels since she hadn't eaten much since her surgery.

As Frankie slept that afternoon, I had so many questions about IVDD. Except for the nurturing care, medication routine, and dog carts, I wasn't given any other information on how to help Frankie walk again. Still feeling helpless and wondering what more I could expect or do, I turned to the Internet to see if I could find more information on helping Frankie make a full recovery.

During my search I discovered an organization called Dodgerslist. The founder, Linda Stowe, created Dodgerslist because of a Dachshund named Dodger. Dodger had IVDD and was euthanized because of the lack of knowledge his owners had of the disease and treatment options available. When Linda heard of this sad story, she immediately went to work to create Dodgerslist with one goal in mind: save dogs' lives! Nine years later, Dodgerslist has members in Australia, New Zealand, Canada, England, Mexico, Spain, Ireland, Slovenia, India, Morocco, South Africa, Dubai, and even one in Hong Kong. As I perused their website, I found stories of other Dachshunds with IVDD. Many walked again. I had tears rolling down my face, for it gave me much hope that Frankie would also make a full recovery.

I discovered many articles relating to the care and treatment options for dogs diagnosed with IVDD. I also discovered a Yahoo group where owners of IVDD dogs could connect, and I signed up immediately. They have very dedicated members who monitor the email-based group, answering questions of other owners who live with and care for IVDD dogs, as well as those looking for answers, like me. I was so relieved and felt a peaceful calm wash over me. Here was a group of people who understood exactly what I was going through.

My research confirmed that Frankie would need six to eight weeks of strict cage rest to give her the best chances of recovery. Dodgerslist advised keeping pets with IVDD immobile to give the spine a chance to fully heal. *How would I keep Frankie crated for that long? Wouldn't she go crazy being cooped up? Would she be lonely?* I wondered.

While I understood how important it was to keep her immobile, I felt bad she had to stay in her small crate almost twenty-four hours a day. I reached out to the Yahoo group and expressed my concern. One of the members suggested getting Frankie a larger, open wired kennel. She said to place it in the room that we are most often in, so Frankie wouldn't feel lonely.

After reading that, I made a quick trip to a local pet store and bought an open wire kennel. When I got home, I decided having it in the kitchen would be the best place, since that is where we spend the majority of our time. Kylie's large kennel was also in our kitchen, so we placed Frankie's kennel on top of Kylie's.

John smiled and said, "It looks like a two-story condominium."

I took Frankie out of her small crate and placed her in the new, larger one. Kylie looked up at Frankie in her kennel, her nose barely reaching the edge of it, and gave Frankie's new home a sniff.

I said, "There you go, Frankie. Kylie is right below you in her condo, so you don't need to be scared or feel alone."

As I looked at Frankie I thought about how she was used to having the run of the house for over six years, as well as snuggling with Kylie the past six months. I didn't know who this was going to be harder on, John and me, or Frankie. But thankfully, we all adjusted pretty quickly.

The next day I continued reading all I could on Dodgerslist website. I learned that physical therapy (PT) was something I could do for Frankie to keep her muscles strong in the event she did walk on her own again. As I researched local facilities that offered PT services, I was disheartened to find out that the closest place in Wisconsin was nearly two hours away from my home. From what I read, PT was recommended twice a day, every day. It was also expensive. I lost a bit of hope discovering this. I knew we couldn't afford the PT, and driving two hours each way every day wasn't going to be feasible.

There was also a top-notch PT facility in Chicago, which some of Dodgerslist members highly recommended. I emailed them about Frankie. They wrote back and told me I would need to leave Frankie with them for about three months so they could work with her every day. I really didn't feel Frankie would do well being away from us and because the cost wasn't something we could afford, I had to let that option go.

This was the hardest part: wanting to do all I could for Frankie and realizing we didn't have the money. It was such a helpless feeling. It brought back feelings of when Cassie had cancer. If chemotherapy had been an option for her, we would have faced the same dilemma because of the exorbitant cost. The only thing that brought me some peace was that even if we could have afforded the PT option, it was not a guarantee that Frankie would walk. I decided to let my thoughts on all this rest for a while.

CHAPTER FOURTEEN

Helping Frankie

A week after being home, Frankie was scheduled to have her stitches removed by Dr. Q, who had originally diagnosed her with IVDD. I shared with him all the information I had learned through Dodgerslist. He was unaware of the organization. I also told him about the physical therapy and explained that we wouldn't be able to do it because of the expense and the distance to the facility.

He said, "I know of a veterinarian at the Pewaukee Clinic that specializes in IVDD. I can give you her information and you may want to set up a consultation with her. I think she may even be able to teach you some PT techniques that you could do for Frankie at home."

I was so happy to hear this news, and eagerly wrote down her name and phone number.

I waited a few more weeks, as I knew crate rest was essential for Frankie, and I wanted to adhere to that as closely as possible. I made an appointment for Frankie to see Dr. M at the Pewaukee Clinic about three weeks after her stitches were removed. Though I was nervous about taking her in the car, I felt it was necessary to find out what more I could do to help her.

My mom agreed to go with me. We drove to Pewaukee on a warm day in May to meet with Dr. M. My hopes were once again high. When we arrived we were taken into an exam room right away. Shortly after, Dr. M entered and introduced herself. She was very soft spoken and kind as she asked about

Frankie. Dr. Q had faxed Frankie's medical information, so she had that sitting in front of her.

She was gentle with Frankie as she examined her. She took an instrument that sort of looked like a pliers and pinched it between Frankie's toes. Frankie didn't flinch or cry out in any pain.

She said, "I'm concerned that at this point she still has no feeling in her back legs. But it is early in the game, so there is still hope."

Next she showed me different types of gentle exercises that I could do for Frankie's paralyzed legs.

She said, "These exercises won't put any pressure on her spine, but will help her regain muscle tone. It's important that muscle atrophy doesn't set in. If she is to walk again you want her muscles to stay strong."

I nodded, watching her move Frankie's leg in a circle clockwise and then counter clockwise. Dr. M showed me a variety of what she called "range of motion" movements. One exercise had me pretending like Frankie was doing knee bends. She held onto Frankie's tiny foot and gently moved her leg towards her belly and then back down. The last exercise she showed me was how to move Frankie's leg as if she was pedaling a bicycle.

I smiled and said, "I have a dog basket on my bike that she loves to ride in. I think she'll enjoy this exercise."

"I suggest doing the exercises twice a day. You'll need to move each of Frankie's legs through the different exercises I showed you and do about one hundred repetitions per leg, per session." She also suggested hydro-therapy. The clinic had a heated pool where they worked with dogs like Frankie to help them strengthen their muscles. But she said I could get a similar effect by helping Frankie swim in the bathtub at home. She also suggested some supplements since Frankie's immune system was compromised from the surgery, weight loss, and the medications she was on. "If Frankie is to regain the use of her back legs you should see some improvement within about three months. You could see something sooner, but give it at least three months. I've also seen cases where dogs go as long as six months before regaining use of their hind legs. So try to hang in there."

We briefly talked about dog carts or wheelchairs, as they are also referred to. But I still was having a hard time considering a wheelchair for Frankie. It wasn't what I wanted for her. I just couldn't imagine her having to live the rest of her life like that. In my heart I wanted more than anything for her to walk on her own two back legs again. It was the only outcome I could accept.

"Thank you so much for all the great information you've given me today. I'm confident I can do the exercises for Frankie. I have a new sense of hope that Frankie is going to be just fine and recover fully from this."

She smiled and said, "You're welcome. Please don't hesitate to call me at anytime with any questions or concerns."

As we left the clinic I was full of renewed hope. I truly believed if I did all that Dr. M told me and taught me that Frankie would soon be walking on her own again. I set my sights on three months at the time when this would happen. Nothing was going to stop me from making that reality come true. Every morning and late afternoon I would lay Frankie on our bed and go through her exercise routine. At the beginning, adjusting and finding time for everything with Frankie seemed daunting. But soon enough we fell into a comfortable routine.

Being with her and helping her little legs become strong again, I felt our bond deepen even more. It made me feel good to know I was doing all I possibly could to help her. I sensed she understood what I was doing and that I was trying to help her heal. Though the first few exercise sessions she didn't seem so sure and would wiggle around as I tried to work on her little legs. But after about three days she would relax the minute I laid her on the bed. I'd begin with her lying on one side and work her leg through all the exercises, and then turn her over and do the other leg. She would often close her eyes as we got into the routine. This made me smile to think she was so content. I came to really enjoy our workout sessions together and found myself relaxing as well.

One of the hardest things to adjust to with Frankie's paralysis was the timing of her bladder and bowel movements. I really thought I was going to lose my mind at the beginning. I couldn't seem to get the hang of when she had to go. It seemed like I was constantly cleaning up pee and poop. There would be times I would get so angry, but then I'd realize Frankie couldn't help it. I'd feel guilty for getting mad. One day I went out for about an hour to run some errands. When I returned home Frankie had once again had a big mess in her kennel. I stood there looking at her and started to cry. I didn't want to do this anymore. I couldn't take it. I was lost in my own pity party, crying and feeling sorry for myself. But all of a sudden I realized something.

Standing alone in my kitchen, I put my hands on my hips and said, "Barb, there are worse things in life than pee and poop." I cried and laughed at the same time as I realized the simplicity of it all and how stressed out it had made me. I realized I had a choice. I could continue to be freaked out every time she made a mess, or I could accept the hand I was dealt. The amazing thing was that when I changed my attitude, the timing of Frankie's bathroom habits seemed to fall into place much better. The more I realized the important role of my attitude, the better things seemed to be. I haven't always been a very patient person, but I was beginning to learn to be more patient.

I continued to research Dodgerslist website for any more information on how I could help Frankie heal. One day I ran across an article on canine massage. I immediately called our library to ask if they had any books on the subject. They had one, so I ran down and picked it up. Following the diagrams in the book, I incorporated a gentle massage at the end of each of Frankie's exercise sessions.

I also learned about canine acupuncture. There were many cases I read about where acupuncture helped pets with IVDD to walk again. I looked for someone in our area who practiced animal acupuncture, but had a hard time finding someone. Living in a small community can be a challenge when it comes to alternative treatment. But I did eventually find a vet in a neighboring city who did acupuncture. Unfortunately, when I called the number of the clinic I was told Dr. T was no longer practicing. I explained to them my situation and asked if they could recommend anyone else.

The receptionist said, "Well, what I can do is pass your name and number along to Dr. T."

I thanked her and was grateful. I prayed he would call.

A few days later I received a call from him. He would turn out to be the calm in the middle of my frantic, emotional storm. He told me he was no longer practicing because of a spinal injury he himself had suffered two years before. As he told me his story, my heart went out to him. He could relate to what Frankie was experiencing. He asked me to share with him more about Frankie and her diagnoses and prognosis. I tried to not get my hopes up too high, but I got the sense he might be open to helping Frankie. After I finished giving him a full report he said, "I may be willing to try this."

I almost started crying, but held it in. He went on to explain the type of acupuncture he did and how it worked. Because he was no longer practicing, he didn't do acupuncture often, and only on a very limited basis. He wanted me to fully understand that the acupuncture could work, but that it also may not. I assured him I understood. But if he was willing to see her and give it a try, I would be open to whatever the outcome was.

He said, "Okay, let's set up a time to meet at the clinic."

Three days later Frankie and I met with Dr. T. I found him to be a soft spoken, kind, and gentle man. Before he did an acupuncture session for her, we talked more about Frankie and all I was doing for her at this point.

"Frankie may not care for the needles," he cautioned me, "and if so, I can't go forward with the procedure. "I'll need complete silence so I can put all my energy into working with Frankie."

I nodded.

It took him a few tries, but Frankie finally relaxed and accepted the needles he was placing in different parts of her body. I breathed a sigh of relief. The whole procedure took about forty-five minutes. When he was done he said, "I can't promise you anything, but I felt Frankie did very well."

"I'm just so thankful you were willing to see us and give this a try. I can't thank you enough."

Dr. T then said something to me that I didn't expect. "I know you are trying everything you know to help Frankie. I commend you for that. But I also want you to realize that you need to take care of yourself too. If you get yourself too stressed out about all of this, you won't be able to take the best care of Frankie."

Tears filled my eyes. He was right. I was on an overload of emotions and exhausted in trying to do all I could for her. In that moment Dr. T gave me one of the best gifts that would help me and Frankie as we moved forward. He gave me permission to know it was okay to take time for me, so I in turn could be there for Frankie.

I whispered, holding back tears, "Thank you."

I picked up Frankie and as we were heading out the door he said, "I'll follow up with you in about a week. If you don't see signs of improvement in Frankie within about a week, it probably means she's not a candidate for further treatments."

"I understand. I'll talk to you in a week."

I held Frankie in my right arm, with my purse hanging over my right shoulder and headed to the receptionist desk to pay for the service. As the receptionist was telling me what I owed for the service, I looked into my purse to find my checkbook. As I did, I wondered what that was that I saw laying in the crease of my checkbook. Upon closer examination, I realized that it was a small turd— Frankie had pooped in my purse!

With a straight face as if nothing strange had occurred, I calmly shook the little turd to the side, took out my checkbook, and proceeded to pay my bill. As Frankie and I headed for the door, it took all I could to not bust out laughing. The minute we were outside, I began laughing so hard that I almost peed in my pants.

Still laughing, I got Frankie settled into her doggie car seat. I couldn't wait to call John to tell him what happened. Dialing my cell phone, and anticipating sharing this funny story with John, I was still laughing so hard and tears were rolling down my cheeks. When he answered I could barely get the story out. When I finally did, we both thought we would never ever stop laughing. Now, I realize some people may totally have freaked out about finding a turd in their purse, but after dealing with all the poop and potty issues of an IVDD dog, it truly was no big deal to me. I was learning to not sweat the small stuff.

The following week Dr. T called to see if Frankie was responding to the treatment. He said, "Have you noticed any movement in her legs or tail?"

"No, everything seems to be the same."

"I'm sorry to hear this."

"I'm truly grateful, Dr. T., that you gave it a try. I can't thank you enough."

We hung up and I thought about what an honor it was to have met him. He was quite the humble man and I don't know if he understood the magnitude of what he did for me when he told me that it was important to take care of myself through all of this. To this day, talking about that moment still brings tears to my eyes.

CHAPTER FIFTEEN

Acceptance

As I continued my physical therapy routine for Frankie, I tried hard to stay hopeful. But as we approached the three-month mark, I started to feel sorry for both of us. Her hind legs showed no signs of movement. I briefly thought about the wheelchair, but I had made my mind up that I didn't want her to have a dog cart. I wanted so badly for her to be a "normal" dog again. I wanted her to walk and run on her own. In short, I had a hard time accepting reality.

One afternoon I had Frankie lying on the bed as I ran through her leg exercises once again. It was an especially difficult day. I started thinking about the many years ahead of having to help Frankie go to the bathroom. I wondered if my husband and I would ever go on vacation again. *Who would want to take care of a handicapped dog?* The thought felt overwhelming, and unfair. I loved her with all my heart and would do anything for her, but thinking about the future was depressing.

I had the TV on for background noise as I was moving Frankie's legs through the exercises. The Oprah show was on, but I wasn't really paying attention. Just as more thoughts of pity started to swirl through my mind, I heard Oprah introduce her next guest. My ears perked up when she said, "Meet Faith, a dog born with only two legs."

As I looked up at the TV, I saw the sweetest and cutest dog hopping across the stage on her rear legs. Her two front legs were just small stubs. As I watched her happily make her way across the stage to Oprah, tears spilled down my cheeks. Not out of pity for Faith, but out of happiness. I listened as Faith's owner, Judy, told the audience how she adopted Faith knowing the dog only had two legs. She talked about how she taught Faith to walk by training her with peanut butter. I was in awe of this remarkable woman and her love for her dog.

It was in that moment that I realized I had a choice. I could continue to feel sorry for myself and Frankie, but what would that change? Something in me shifted and I knew that it was up to me to look for the blessing in why this had happened. My eyes blurred with tears, I looked down at Frankie. She was looking back at me with her soft brown eyes. It occurred to me in that moment that Frankie didn't feel sorry for herself. She never had. She simply adjusted and was going on with her life. She was being positive in the face of a challenge. I realized I needed to do the same and made my mind up to do just that.

A few days later I called Dr. M at the Pewaukee Clinic to touch base with her about Frankie's progress—or lack of it at this point.

"I'm at a loss of what to do," I said.

She said, "Well, you might want to consider a dog cart for Frankie."

This time I was ready to hear what she had to say. Dr. M told me that sometimes dogs can still gain back full mobility after using a dog cart for a few weeks or months. She couldn't guarantee this would be the case with Frankie, but nonetheless a dog cart would give her the freedom to run and play again. Even if she never regained the use of her back legs, she would still be able to do all the dog things she did before. Dr. M didn't recommend one specific company, but told me there were various wheelchair companies on the Internet that I could research. I was eager to get started.

After talking with Dr. M, I immediately got on my computer and started looking for dog cart companies. I found five different ones. Some dog carts were adjustable and some were custom-made. The company that caught my eye was Eddie's Wheels based out of Shelburne Falls, Massachusetts. As I delved further into their website I discovered the CEO of their company is Daisy, a little red, smooth dachshund that looked very much like Frankie. As you may have guessed by now, I cry easily, so yes, tears sprang to my eyes seeing this adorable little dog on wheels. The spunky look on her face grabbed a hold of my heart. I just knew this was the company I would work with to customize a wheelchair for Frankie.

As I read about Eddie and Leslie Grinnell, I fell in love with their story. Eddie began the company years ago because a dog he had at the time had suffered a back injury. His vet told him the best thing to do was put the dog to sleep. Eddie would hear nothing of it. Being an engineer by trade, he went home and designed a wheelchair for his dog to help him walk. He shared his idea with his vet, who said it would never work. But the dog went on to live a long, happy, quality life. The vet was amazed and started referring clients with dogs who had similar problems to Eddie. Realizing he could help many more dogs, Eddie's Wheels was born. They make 1,500 to 2,000 wheelchairs a year.

I picked up the phone and called their company. Leslie answered. I explained to her Frankie's IVDD and prognosis. They have made many wheelchairs for Dachshunds with IVDD, so she was familiar with the disease. She said, "The wheelchair we will design for Frankie will work in such a way that it is physical therapy for her. With regular use, and overtime, Frankie may learn to pick up her back feet while walking in her dog cart, and may eventually walk on her own without the help of the cart."

I was hopeful that maybe this could happen for Frankie. But I also was finally in a place that I accepted that Frankie could be in the dog cart for the duration of her life. No matter what, I was excited to know that she would soon be a normal dog again, able to run, walk, and play.

Leslie said, "You'll need to take certain measurements of Frankie so her wheelchair will fit her just right, and support her spine. You'll need to measure from the base of her neck to the base of her tail, around her chest, her waist, and then from the top of her belly to the bottom of the floor. The directions and a diagram are on our website to help guide you. Once you send us the measurements it will take about three weeks to make Frankie's dog cart and ship it out to you."

I thanked her for all her help and told her I'd be in touch soon. The following day I emailed her Frankie's measurements.

Just as they promised, Frankie's dog cart arrived three weeks later. It was the middle of July when the UPS truck pulled up in front of our house with Frankie's special delivery. I could hardly contain my excitement as I ran outside to greet the UPS driver. When I got back in the house I set the box on the kitchen table. Frankie and John were next to me as I opened it. As I looked inside I saw Frankie's brand new, shiny wheels. Tears of joy sprang to my eyes.

I looked down at Frankie and saw her looking at me. I said, "Frankie, these are your wheels! Now you will be able to run and play, and chase bunnies and squirrels again." As I took the wheelchair out of the box, I looked at John and smiled. I said, "Wow, open box, take out wheelchair, insert dog, and watch her run!" He laughed.

I scooped Frankie under my arm, and with the wheelchair in my other hand, I headed out to the front yard. I took out the two metal pins that hold the wheelchair together. Then I unbuckled the harness which would go around the front of Frankie's chest. I placed Frankie's back legs in the two openings on the back of the wheelchair. Then I closed the bar over the top of her and placed the metal pins into place to close the wheelchair and that would keep Frankie's back straight and aligned within it. The last step was putting the harness around the front of her chest and snapping it into place.

As soon as I had her in her wheels, I kneeled down at her side and said, "Run free, Frankie! I know you can do it!"

She didn't move an inch. She looked at me and just stood there. It was as if she was a statue. I thought, *oh no! Now what am I going to do?* I didn't realize that, of course, Frankie had never had a wheelchair. This was all new to her. She didn't know what to do. I sat next to her, wondering how I was going to train her to walk in her wheels. Then an idea came to me! I jumped up and ran into the house and grabbed a handful of dog treats. I also thought being in the grass might be hard for her to get going so I placed her on the street in front of our house. Then I placed a treat every few inches apart on the pavement.

It took only a few moments and all of a sudden Frankie began to move toward the first treat. Once she had it gobbled it down, onto the next one she went. Once the treats on the street were gone, I held a treat in my hand and she followed along beside me. I encouraged her every step of the way. Before I knew it, we were all the way to the end of the block. I was ecstatic watching her walk again! All the heartache and pain of the past three months melted away as I watched my sweet little dog have her life back. Though I never experienced the joy of my own child walking for the first time, watching Frankie learn to walk in a new way made my heart sing. I was so proud.

As Frankie neared the park on the corner of our block some of the neighborhood boys were playing. For a moment I felt fear rise up in me. I wondered, *would they make fun of Frankie in her wheelchair?* I felt fiercely protective of her and wanted to scoop her up and run home with her before any harm came to her. But I was pleasantly surprised when one of the boys named Travis turned to the other boys, he pointed to Frankie, and yelled enthusiastically, "Hey look! That dog has tires!"

I smiled and felt my heart melt. Not realizing it was a wheelchair, he called it just like he saw it. I thought it was endearing. It would be my first encounter with children, sharing with them why Frankie was in a doggie wheelchair. But as I would come to find out over the next few months, it wouldn't be my last.

CHAPTER SIXTEEN

Dog on Wheels

It took some getting used to for Frankie to maneuver around the house in her cart. For the first couple of weeks she would often get her wheels stuck on a piece of furniture. If I wasn't in the room I would hear her whimpering and go looking for her. Frankie didn't quite know how to put her wheelchair in reverse either. But one day, she finally got the hang of it. The first time she backed up, John and I were able to witness it together.

I said, "Way to go, Frankie! You did it."

John relating it to a big truck backing up said, "Beep. Beep. Beep."

We laughed really hard.

Frankie didn't seem to understand that she now had wheels as her hind legs. All she knew was that she was now able to move about like she used to. Before she had her wheelchair and while she was healing, I left her in her kennel when I was gone. But even with her wheelchair, I was too nervous to leave her in it unattended, so she continued to go in her kennel when I had to leave the house. But one day I was just going to run to the post office in town, which was only three minutes away. I decided to leave her in her dog cart.

When I returned home less than a half hour later she wasn't at the door to greet me— this was unusual. I called her name thinking she was stuck somewhere, but didn't hear anything. I looked all around but couldn't find her anywhere. I began to panic.

I called out, "Frankie! Frankie! Where are you?"

Then I heard the faintest of a whimper. I realized it was coming from downstairs.

We have an opening to our downstairs family room off our kitchen with no door. As I looked to the bottom of the carpeted stairs, I saw Frankie upside down in her wheelchair, the wheels slowly turning. I rushed down to her, crying, "Please, Frankie! Please be okay!"

When I got to her, she was just fine, and didn't seem to be any worse for the wear. I carried her back up the steps, set her down, and off she went as if nothing had happened. I could have kicked myself for not realizing she may try and go down the stairs. She didn't know any better. Within days, I had a baby gate put across the opening so that wouldn't happen again.

Even though Frankie was happy in her wheelchair and adjusting to life on wheels, I was apprehensive about taking her out in public. It isn't every day that you see a dog in a wheelchair in my small community of 900 people, or in our surrounding county, for that matter. I knew it wasn't fair to keep Frankie locked up in our home. I wanted her to be a normal dog and do all the things she had done before. But the fear of what others would think of me was looming large in my mind. I was scared that people would think it was mean of me to have my dog in a wheelchair. All my life I had worried what others thought of me. At times it was painful how much I worried about it. I wanted everyone to like me. But having others accept or like me meant I wasn't always being honest to who I was. It was a miserable way to feel and I didn't want to live like that anymore. I wanted to be comfortable in my own skin and live from my own truth. I didn't want to worry anymore what others thought of me or how they felt I should live my life.

A few days later I was watching Frankie spin her way through the grass, as happy as could be, when something really struck me: Frankie didn't care that she was in a wheelchair. All that mattered to her was that she could get around and be a dog. She was living life to the fullest. In that moment, I realized I had an opportunity to stand tall in who I was and not be afraid of what others thought. I knew deep in my heart I made the right choice for Frankie. She was happy and her quality of life was wonderful. I also realized I was being given the gift of sharing Frankie with others. I could teach them that she was still able to enjoy herself, despite having lost the use of her hind legs. Though I still had some apprehension, Frankie inspired me to move past the fear of taking her into town. I reminded myself that she wasn't worried what others thought about her. I knew I had to do the same.

For our first outing, I decided to take her to our local farmer's and artisan's market, which was held downtown every Saturday morning during the summer months. Before she was diagnosed with IVDD, I'd get out my red bike with my special dog basket that fit over the front of my handlebars. Frankie loves to ride in her basket and we'd head downtown to peruse the market. People always got a kick out of seeing Frankie riding in the basket, especially the way her ears glide straight out to the side when it's windy.

I got out my bike again and put Frankie's wheelchair over my handlebar. Then I strapped Frankie in her basket, and with butterflies in my stomach, we headed to the market. As we approached the market, everyone smiled when they saw Frankie. When we arrived, I parked and got Frankie out of the basket. I placed her in her wheels and started walking around the market. I didn't realize what a show stopper Frankie was going to be. Every few feet I was stopped by someone asking what had happened to her. I was telling her story over and over again that morning.

Many people said, "Bless you for taking care of her and doing what you did to help her." I never expected that, and the fear in me started to subside. There were a few stares from others that made me feel uncomfortable, but I tried my best to move past my fear of those stares. It wasn't easy when I felt their judgment—real or imagined–creep back into my mind.

I didn't get much shopping done at the market that day, which was fine. I was happy that people were so accepting and inspired by my little dog on wheels. What was even better was the reaction of children. I'd watch their faces as they spotted Frankie. Their eyes got as big as saucers and they came running to see her. I shared Frankie's story with many children and it warmed my heart how accepting they were of her.

Someone asked, "Does it hurt?"

"No, Frankie doesn't feel anything in her back and her back legs—she isn't in any pain." Then I'd add, "Isn't it cool that she has wheels that can help her walk?"

The kids nodded enthusiastically. If they weren't with their parents they would jump up and run to find them. I'd hear them yelling, "Mom! Mom! You have to come see the dog with wheels!"

Our first adventure out proved to be a very positive experience. I was relieved. Along with watching Frankie persevere and strut her stuff through the market that day, my confidence in myself began to grow also. I still wasn't sure what the blessing of all this was, but I kept an open mind. Frankie was continually teaching me that staying positive in the face of challenges helped make those challenges a little easier to deal with.

More and more people learned about Frankie as I continued to take her to the farmer's market. Every time someone would hear her story and thank me for helping her, I would feel so good knowing I was bringing a positive face to pets with special needs.

CHAPTER SEVENTEEN

Discovering My Purpose

As winter approached, I decided to attend a writer's conference at a university not far from my home. It would be the first time I left Frankie for a whole weekend, but while I knew it was going to be hard, I wanted so badly to continue my writing. I was attending the conference because I had an idea for an adult nonfiction book about my life with Cassie, and now Frankie, and what I had learned from them.

John agreed to look after Frankie so I could attend the conference. It was amazing to connect with other writers. It was also fun sharing our book ideas and learning from all the different presenters. I was nervous about the publishing process and quite intimidated when I sat in on a panel discussion with editors from New York. When it ended, I walked out, thinking there was no way I could ever have a book published. The process seemed daunting.

The following day I attended a class on independent publishing. As the presenter went through the process, I began to believe that I too could publish my own book. I left the class feeling empowered and inspired, and ready to pursue my project.

As I drove home Sunday afternoon I was on cloud nine, and when I went to bed that night I could barely sleep, with all the wonderful ideas swirling through my mind.

When I awoke Monday morning, John was already gone for the day. I laid there for a few moments, thinking about the conference. All of a sudden I sat straight up in bed and said, "I'm going to write a children's book and it's going to be about Frankie." I was a bit surprised and wondered, *where did that come from?* That was the furthest thing from my mind. But all I can say is that sometimes Divine intervention steps in, and we can either ignore it, or follow it. I chose to follow it. Though I wasn't sure the direction I was headed, I couldn't resist the urge to start that very day. As I began my research on writing a children's book, I knew that if I trusted God, He would guide me.

I was also part of a women's writing group that met every Thursday evening. I loved being a part of it. At our next gathering I announced my book idea. They all rallied around me with resounding encouragement and were very excited for me.

For the remainder of the winter and into spring and early summer I worked diligently on my book. I was really enjoying the process, though I had doubts about whether I was really "qualified" to write a book.

Before I knew it, the farmer's market was once again in full swing. The summer before, I had found it difficult to balance Frankie's wheelchair on my handlebar and brought this up to John. He suggested a carrier on the back of my bike. I purchased a wooden crate and painted it my favorite color, periwinkle. John installed it and it was perfect for holding Frankie's wheelchair, as well as to hold items I bought while at the market.

Frankie is quite the cute sight to see in her wheels, which I was growing accustomed to. I came to accept I wouldn't get much shopping done while at the market. But I was so happy when we ran into new people shopping the market, because I could educate them about the options we have for pets with disabilities. I took great joy and pride in sharing Frankie's story, for I knew it would help others who found themselves facing the same situation.

As we made our way through the market one day, a little boy who looked to be about nine years old saw Frankie and stopped me to ask about her. I explained to him that Frankie has a disc disease which caused paralysis in her back legs. I told him about her wheelchair and how it is similar to a wheelchair for people, and that it helps her to get around. He put his hand on her back and rubbed her spine where it stuck out a little from muscle atrophy.

He said, "Why does it stick out here?"

"Well, that is where the vet had to go in and do surgery. Because Frankie lost some weight from that, her muscles shrunk, so it caused her spine to stick out a little bit."

He put his hand on my shoulder, looked at me and said most confidently, "Well it doesn't matter what you look like on the outside, but what's on the inside."

I looked at him in complete awe and tears pooled in my eyes. I said, "You know what young man? You are absolutely right."

He smiled and walked away.

I sat there for a moment, stunned. I truly believe he was an angel sent from God, because something powerful happened. It was then that I realized the full blessing of all the difficulties of the past few months. For all the doubts I was having about publishing Frankie's story, I believed without a doubt that I truly was meant to write her story and share it with children. I believed with all my heart I was meant to help children see their challenges in a positive way through Frankie's example. That little boy gave me the shot of confidence I needed.

As I continued working on Frankie's book, I still occasionally found myself doubting my capabilities. At times I also still had a battle going on in my head, saying that I wasn't good enough. A lot of writers I knew had a degree in writing and it concerned me that I didn't. I wondered whether anyone would take me seriously.

One day I finally got tired of the constant negative talk in my head. After thinking yet again that there was no way I could do this, I felt this little nudge in my heart. I thought, okay Barb, you may not know everything there is about writing, publishing, and marketing this book, or if anyone will even buy it—but if you don't do this, will you regret it at the end of your life? My eyes stung with tears. I knew the answer. I no longer wanted to listen to my head; I wanted to listen to my heart. There was no way I was going to face myself at the end of my life if I didn't *at least* continue on with this and give it my best. I also knew if I could affect just one child's life with Frankie's story that this would all be worth it. From that day forward, I had few moments of doubt.

By the end of June, I had the first draft of *Frankie the Walk 'N Roll Dog* complete. I was ecstatic! Next came editing, illustrations, layout, and then the final step of having the book printed. Everything was falling into place; and my excitement of seeing my first book published was such an amazing time. It truly felt like I was giving birth. This book was my child and my heart.

I learned every step of the way and felt such pride in each step I took. I could feel myself growing taller in spirit and confidence. Frankie was, and still is, my constant inspiration. On days I felt like I couldn't take the next step, I'd watch her wheeling around in her wheelchair so full of joy, or snoozing contently in my writing cottage, and it would remind me I could do anything I set my mind to do.

As I began to live more and more in my truth, there were times I felt incredibly lonely. Even though this was an exciting time for me, I felt pangs of what used to be and the loss of relationships I had gently let go because they no longer fit with who I was. I had worked so hard in my coaching with Diane to find what brought me joy and I continued to live my life in the way I chose, instead of doing what others expected of me. Though it wasn't always easy, Frankie's spunk for life was my daily reminder for me that I was on the right path.

I found myself having to create boundaries so I didn't go back to my old patterns of thinking or being. Coach Diane had taught me that this was necessary for my own self-care and for me to continue to grow and be the best I could be. The more positive I became, the harder I found it to be around those who were negative. What made it difficult was that some of these people had been in my life for years. I felt bad that I found it challenging to be around them, and I struggled with this for quite some time. I wanted everyone I knew to have the same positive outlook as I did— to know that we each have a choice to be positive when faced with difficulties in our lives. Also, because I found joy in my new path, I wanted everyone to experience this same joy. As bad as I wanted this for those that I loved or cared about, I came to realize that we are each in a different place and on different paths. No path is right or wrong. It was then that I realized that people who challenge me are actually teachers in my life. It isn't that they were "different"—they just have fears of their own, which can sometimes come out in a negative way. But once I understood they were teaching me what I didn't want for my own life, I was grateful for the reminders.

For most of my adult life I have played what I call "small." I've generally been a pretty happy person, but would find myself constricting that joy around those who are unhappy. In my twenties and thirties, I often got so wrapped up in other people's personal dramas that it emotionally affected me. I'd desperately want to take away their pain, but would often do it at the cost of my own emotions and it would leave me feeling drained. As I grew older, I learned to not take in the emotional drama of others, but I still struggled with playing small in some situations. It really came to a head when I began letting friends and family know I had written a children's book and would soon be publishing it. I had kept it a secret from almost everyone until I felt confident enough to share. I knew how my mind worked, and if anyone would have said something negative, or tried to squish my dream, I may have caved in and reverted back to my old ways of thinking. It's sad, but unfortunately not everyone will always support our dreams. I don't believe it's because they don't want to. But speaking from personal experience, what comes up sometimes is our own unlived dreams. I can't tell you how many times in the past I've been jealous of someone else doing something I wished I had had the courage to do. But I now realize when others can't feel joy for you, it isn't that they don't want to; they may not know how, or are simply not ready.

As I was taking steps to live a happier life, I found that it was sometimes hard work. Digging deep into one's soul is not an easy thing to do. But I feel incredibly blessed that I found the courage to start being me. My dogs, especially Frankie, were instrumental in helping me with this. And Kylie? Well, Kylie loves to watch the world go by through the view of the open front door. It used to bother me that she isn't a typical Lab who likes to play ball or go swimming. But in learning to accept her for who she is, this reminds me to accept myself for who I am.

Another thing that has helped keep me on my spiritual path is reading motivational and inspirational books. I'm also a fan of Hay House Radio. I love their motto, "Radio for Your Soul." One of my favorite speakers on the spiritual radio show is Dr. Wayne Dyer. I remember the summer I was writing Frankie's book as a glorious time. I was learning to let the self doubt that would creep in now and then move through my mind without giving it too much attention. I was learning to let it go. Listening to Dr. Wayne Dyer, as well as other talk show hosts on Hay House, always helped me stay on a positive track. I also downloaded Hay House Radio on my iPod and listened to it on my morning walks.

One morning a person called in to Dr. Dyer's show and asked, "How do you find your purpose?"

Dr. Dyer said, "I don't believe you find your purpose, but your purpose finds you."

My breath caught in my chest and tears slowly rolled down my cheeks as I walked through our small town early that morning. It struck me deeply because it was exactly what happened to me. I could attest to the fact that if we are open to blessings and opportunities, unexpected and wonderful things can happen. Hearing Dr. Dyer talk about purpose reaffirmed for me that I had found mine.

CHAPTER EIGHTEEN

Giving Birth

January 11, 2008 is a day I'll never forget. I was about to give birth. I eagerly waited that morning for the freight truck carrying my precious cargo to arrive. I was nervous, scared, and happy all at the same time. I actually thought I might jump out of my own skin! One thousand copies of my first children's book were on their way and I was nervous that they might not sell. I was scared that maybe the books wouldn't turn out as I had planned and imagined. But most of all, I was happy I had done what I set out to do: I had written and published my own book.

As I heard the truck rumble down our dead-end road, the butterflies in my stomach really began to flutter. I was on the verge of crying, mostly from excitement. As the driver pulled up and got out of the truck, I was too nervous to go out and greet him, so John did. I watched from the window as the driver slowly lowered the lift on the truck that lowered my pallet of books to the ground.

I saw John point to our open garage as the driver wheeled the load down the driveway. It seemed like forever for him to finally make his way back to the truck. When I saw him beginning to raise the lift again, I couldn't stand the anticipation any longer. With a box cutter in hand, I opened the back door and rushed into the garage. My hands were shaking as I cut open the first box. I prayed with all my heart that the printed version would be what I was expecting. I had just invested all our vacation money and there was no turning back now.

As I pulled out a copy of *Frankie the Walk 'N Roll Dog* I ran my hand across the cover. It was perfect. Nervously, I began to turn the pages to be sure they were all there and looked like I had planned. Then the tears came as I realized I had accomplished my dream of writing this book. It's hard to explain in words and express what that moment meant to me, but it was a feeling I had never experienced before. All the months of uncertainty when Frankie was diagnosed with IVDD, to accepting our fate, and then realizing this was my purpose is hard to grasp in adequate words. In my hands I held what I came to call "my heart." Within the pages of my writing lay a path I had never imagined for myself. The blessing of it all was now here, clear as day and the blessings would continue to blossom.

Now that my book was published, I came to discover that the hard work was just beginning. At times I have shared with others that if someone would have told me the amount of hard work that marketing truly is, I might have run the other way. But I had one thing that was going to drive me, keep me confident, and believe I was meant to share Frankie's story—passion—as well as my biggest inspiration, Frankie.

As I started to put myself out into the world, I would sometimes think back to when I was trying to set up appointments with doctors or potential team members as a nutriceutical consultant. I remember being sick to my stomach and doing anything I could to procrastinate to not have to make those cold calls. But something was very different with promoting myself to schools and libraries with my book. Yes, I was still nervous, and would have tons of butterflies flying around in my stomach, but I *wanted* to share Frankie's story. I *had* to share Frankie's story. And I *believed* with every fiber of my being that it's what I was brought here to do. This was all so new to me. I had never felt like this and had never experienced this *knowing*. But now that I had, I vowed I would do all I could to keep living this way. It felt incredibly good. I never wanted to lose how right this felt.

As I began booking school and library visits with Frankie, the blessings came one right after another. During the first year I was so nervous before each presentation, but felt this incredible high after I was done. Watching the kids react to Frankie in such a positive way was all I needed to keep going. After my presentation kids lined up to pet Frankie, and they'd often say, "Frankie, you're so brave" or "Frankie, you inspire me" or "Frankie, I love you." Frankie was having a huge impact on children and it became the most rewarding work I'd ever done in my life.

As Frankie and I visited more and more schools, it had me often thinking back to when I was a young girl and how insecure I was. Now when I stand in front of a room of children, with Frankie beside me, I want more than anything for kids to feel good about themselves. It's my hope that we help children see their challenges in a positive way. I try to help them understand, that like Frankie, they too will have obstacles throughout their lives. But they always have a choice. They can be negative or positive when facing challenges. I encourage them to choose the positive path and to look for blessings despite hardships. I feel confident sharing this message with them because it's truly what Frankie has taught me.

I remember how my whole outlook changed the day I realized I could continue to be sad that Frankie could no longer walk, or I could change my attitude and be thankful she was alive and thriving. I witnessed first-hand how choosing to be positive and looking for the blessing in our situation changed everything. Knowing this gave me the confidence every time I shared Frankie's story not only with children, but adults as well.

I would also be tested to stand in my truth, as more and more people learned about me and my book. Because I was active in social media, promoting a positive message about pets with special needs, I wasn't always met with those who agreed. One day I received a friend request on Facebook from a Dachshund breeder in Scotland. After accepting her friend request, she emailed me to tell me that she thought it was very selfish of me to have kept Frankie alive. She told me that it wasn't natural to have to help a pet go to the bathroom. She also told me that forcing Frankie to be in a wheelchair was cruel. My initial reaction was anger. I thought, how dare she tell me that I was selfish! She didn't know me or know Frankie. How could she make such a judgment? But I realized then that I was also judging her. Perhaps she wasn't educated about IVDD. I thought, *I have another chance to educate someone else.* I approached emailing her with a positive attitude, hoping to help her understand that dogs with IVDD can, and do, live quality lives. Unfortunately, I learned that most people understand, but some do not. After a few emails back and forth I could see I wasn't going to change her mind. But it taught me that I knew in my heart I did the right thing for Frankie and that was all that mattered. I know I wasn't selfish.

I also recall doing my first TV interview when the host asked me, "What is one of the biggest lessons Frankie has taught you?"

I said, "She has given me a confidence I never had before."

The host seemed surprised, "She gave you confidence?"

"Yes, I used to be very shy, but when all this happened to Frankie and I decided to write her story, I knew I'd have to speak in front of an audience and that really scared me. But, I'm passionate about sharing Frankie's message. I also understood I could be met with those who don't agree that putting a dog in a wheelchair is the right thing to do. But it didn't matter, because I knew in my heart this message needed to be shared. This helped take away much of my fear and the more I get out there and share my message, the more confident I get."

As I drove home from the interview, I thought about when I was in my twenties and thirties and how painfully shy I was. It was hard to go out in public and just strike up a conversation with people I didn't know. Before John and I would leave our home to go out into a social setting, I'd have to have a glass of wine in order to feel more comfortable. I didn't consider myself having a problem with drinking, but this just seemed to help take the edge off. It bothered me that I had to have a drink before going out, but it was the only thing then that helped me feel more at ease. As I did more and more talks with Frankie, I found that I no longer needed that glass of wine. What really helped was that I was being asked to speak to organizations such as Lion's Clubs, women's groups, et cetera. Some of these events were held in the evening, and it just didn't seem right to have a glass of wine before my presentation. I wanted to be the best I could be, and leave a positive impact on my audience. Public speaking is often cited as peoples' number one fear, and doing it helped me overcome my other fears of inadequacy. This led me to believing more and more in me, and much of my shyness has faded away.

In December I was contacted by third grade teacher, Julie, at Longfellow Elementary school. A friend had given her my book at a dinner party, and she had sat in a corner and read it cover to cover. She enjoyed every moment of it, she said, and asked if I'd come visit her classroom and share Frankie's story with her students.

Julie is a kind, petite lady, and an incredibly wonderful teacher. The day we visited her classroom, she warmly welcomed us and confidently handed her classroom over to me. When I was done with my presentation and packing up my suitcase she said, "Frankie is so good with the children. Have you ever thought about training her to be a therapy dog?"

Looking down so she couldn't see the tears that swam in my eyes, I said, "No I've never thought about that. I was actually training my yellow Lab to be my therapy dog when Frankie got hurt. I put everything on hold to take care of Frankie." I shared with her how sad I was when I realized it was likely I wouldn't have a therapy dog for some time to come.

"Well, I think Frankie would be a great therapy dog. She is so calm and accepting of all the children petting her."

I listened intently as she told me that she had just sent in her test to Therapy Dogs Inc. and was waiting to hear whether she qualified to become a tester for them. I wasn't so sure Frankie would be a good therapy dog. I said, "I've never done any formal training with Frankie. I'm not so sure she could pass the required test."

"I'd be happy to work with you and Frankie to help you become a team."

"Do you really think we could become a team?"

She smiled and nodded. "My dog, Preston, is a therapy dog. I'll keep in touch with you and let you know when I hear back from Therapy Dogs Inc. and then we can set up a time to meet."

I didn't want to get my hopes up too high, but excitedly said, "Thank you so much. It would be wonderful if Frankie passed the test."

"Don't worry. She will. I have no doubt."

I drove home excited about a new adventure with Frankie. And then I remembered my mom's words of wisdom the night Frankie got hurt: "Maybe Frankie is meant to be your therapy dog." It occurred to me how Frankie was first a therapy dog for me, helping me become stronger in who I am, and now there was a wonderful possibility that she would become a therapy dog for others. My mom's wise words were coming true.

CHAPTER NINETEEN

Making a Difference

In May, Julie called to tell me that she had passed her test with flying colors and was now an official tester with Therapy Dogs Inc. She also told me she would first need to finish out the school year before she had time to start working with Frankie and me. I could hardly wait for June to arrive.

It was a cool June day when Julie came to my house to do some preliminary testing with Frankie and me. She brought along a copy of the test and a list of requirements Frankie would need to pass in order to become a therapy dog. I giggled when I read that one of the commands she would need to do is, sit.

Smiling I said, "I don't think Frankie will be able to do that too well."

"Don't worry about that too much," Julie giggled.

As we ran Frankie through the different exercises on the test, she did well. When we were done Julie and I sat on the grass with her dog Preston, who had waited patiently in the car until we were finished.

Julie said, "One of the most important parts of the test is that Frankie takes her lead from you. She did that for each of the points on the test. I don't see a problem with her becoming a therapy dog."

"Really? Oh, I'm so excited! This is going to be great fun."

Our next testing phase was to visit a nursing home three different times to see how Frankie reacted around others. We chose a facility Preston and Julie visit often. It was my hope to take Frankie to nursing homes once she became a registered therapy dog, so this seemed like a good fit.

Our first visit to the nursing home was in mid-July. This particular nursing home caught me off guard as we made our way through the facility. It wasn't what I expected. It wasn't well lit and many of the residents seemed to be on many medications. Many were not responsive. Some had dried food on their faces, or on their clothing. Some sat in wheelchairs, drooling. It was incredibly hard to see, and it was very depressing. I drove home that day thinking I may not follow through with becoming a therapy dog team.

Though I couldn't shake some of the images of the residents from my mind, I decided to give it another try. One thing I observed on our visits was how Frankie didn't judge or seem to have an issue with any of the things that bothered me. She would roll happily into a room, ready to make someone's day, no matter what. I decided if she could do it, so could I.

After our second visit, Julie commented on how caring I was with the residents. She said, "When we test a dog to become a therapy dog we are not only testing the dog, but testing the handler as well. We test them for compassion and empathy. You have those qualities."

"Wow, thank you so much, Julie. That makes me feel really good."

While Frankie and I were still in our testing phase, I heard of a new assisted living facility called Libby's House that was looking for a therapy dog. Even though Frankie had not yet passed all the testing, I called and spoke to the activity director. She knew of Frankie because of the local news coverage I had gotten with my book about her, so she was thrilled to hear from me. She said that as soon as I was ready to just give her a call. She would be waiting for me.

Our last day of testing was on a warm and humid August day. The residents we visited lived on the fourth floor so we took the elevator up. Frankie was not too crazy about elevators and didn't like getting onto them. As the elevator opened, Frankie stood near the edge, not sure about rolling out. As I looked up, waiting for Frankie to exit the elevator, I saw a man in a wheelchair. His face lit up when he saw Frankie.

He said, "Well what do we have here?" Then with a concerned look he said, "What happened to you, little pup?"

"Frankie has a disc disease that caused paralysis in her hind legs."

He smiled, and with tears in his eyes, he said, "You have wheels, just like me."

Julie and I looked at each other. It was truly a touching moment. The connection between the sweet elderly man and Frankie was palpable.

"I said, "Yes, she does. And she loves visiting here."

He reached down and petting the top of her head said, "Well, you just made my day."

Smiling I said, "You are so welcome. We will see you later."

As we made our rounds that day I felt myself becoming more and more comfortable around the ailing residents. It felt good to know Frankie and I were bringing a small bit of joy to their days.

When we were done we all headed back down to the elevator. As we rode down, Julie smiled and told us what a great team we were going to make. I was thrilled! I looked at Julie and realized that it seemed as if something was different about her. She had looked like she had gained some weight, though I didn't want to say anything. But it was quite noticeable on her petite frame.

I said, "Something seems different about you today."

She got the biggest smile on her face and said, "I'm pregnant."

"That's wonderful. Congratulations!"

When we got to the first floor, we made our way outside and we sat on the front lawn with the dogs beside us. I watched as Julie signed the certificate that now solidified that Frankie and I were a registered therapy dog team. My dream of having a therapy dog had come true. I was so happy. As the months went by, Julie and I became dear friends. I learned that she and her husband had tried for years to have a baby. They had given up hope earlier that year, and Julie had finally accepted that as her fate. It was so moving to me that in the midst of accepting she would never have children, and then focusing on the needs of helping others, Julie finally became pregnant. It was another shining example of acceptance and moving forward despite one's personal plans that the true plan would be revealed. This lesson didn't go unnoticed between Julie and me; it brought a special meaning to our friendship.

A few weeks after Frankie and I were officially a therapy dog team, we began to visit Libby's House. Many of the residents have Alzheimer's or dementia. I found myself once again feeling uncomfortable around residents who seemed to talk in circles, not really making any sense, or had no concept of what I might be saying to them. But what I did come to see and realize, is that even though they seemed to be living in their own little world, and most likely not close to any resemblance of who they used to be, they were still "in there." They were still human beings with feelings and emotions.

On one of our first visits, we met a delightful man in his early 70s who stole my heart from the moment I met him. Patty, the activity director, had first introduced us to the residents who were gathered together in the large living room. I spent some time taking Frankie around to each of them so they could pet her.

After we were done Patty said, "Would you mind stopping by Daniel's room? I have a feeling he would like to meet Frankie. He loves dogs."

"Sure, of course."

We headed down the hallway. As Patty walked into Daniel's room we followed behind. Patty said, "Daniel, I have someone very special for you to meet."

Daniel was sitting on his bed, listening to music from days gone by. He smiled. He was holding an oversized, stuffed yellow Lab on his lap. A lump caught in my throat seeing the sweet image of this.

Patty said, "Daniel, I want you to meet Frankie, a little dog on wheels."

Daniel continued to smile, still looking at Patty. He didn't seem to understand. Patty said, "Daniel, look down. This is Frankie, a special dog that has come to visit you."

As Daniel glanced down to the floor, still looking puzzled, he caught his first glimpse of Frankie. The biggest, warmest smile filled Daniel's whole face as his eyes met Frankie's. He quickly set the stuffed dog to the side and got down on his hands and knees. He didn't say a word, but the happiness on his face told it all as he began petting Frankie. Then he laid down next to Frankie and began hugging and kissing her.

Patty said, "Daniel, isn't she special?"

Daniel nodded and kept petting Frankie. I was overcome with emotion by this point. My throat hurt from trying not to cry, and I was trying desperately to hold back the tears. I was sitting on the floor next to Frankie as I looked up at Patty, tears now filling my eyes. I put my hand on my heart and whispered, "This is what it's all about."

Patty's eyes were misty too as she nodded.

After a few minutes, Patty said, "Daniel, Frankie will come visit you again, okay?"

He nodded, stood up and sat back down on his bed.

I said, "Goodbye, Daniel. I promise to bring Frankie again to visit with you."

He smiled and starting humming along to the radio.

A few days later, as I was running an errand, I thought about how good I felt while doing therapy work with Frankie at Libby's house. I felt like I now had all these surrogate grandparents. My own grandparents were all gone. My Grandma P, with whom I spent a lot of time when I was younger, was my last grandma to pass away. She ended up in a nursing home, and towards the end of her life had a hard time remembering family and friends. The last visit I had with her she was heavily medicated. I struggled with seeing her like that. After that day, she declined rapidly. I remember my dad calling me a few days later saying that Grandma P was not doing well. I couldn't bear to bring myself to go see her. I would live with that guilt for a long time after she passed. As I drove down the highway thinking about all of this after having met Daniel, I started to cry. I asked my grandma to please forgive me for not coming to see her in her final days. I told her about my therapy work with Frankie. All of a sudden I felt this warmth enfold me and I felt a sense of peace. I truly believe it was my grandma's way of letting me know she loved me, and it was okay.

As Frankie and I continued to visit Libby's House, I formed special friendships with many of them. Frankie would lie on the resident's laps or lay at their feet. After several visits I realized that all they want is for someone to listen to them, or just be with them. It still sometimes makes me sad to see residents in distress, confused, and unaware. And it's hard to think about what may lay ahead for people I've grown close to. But whenever I need strength to deal with it, I take my cue from the friends I have made at Libby's House, and Frankie, as reminders to live each day to the fullest.

Each time we visited, I first and foremost sought out Daniel. I had grown very fond of him. Patty had shared with me that Daniel had been a crime scene investigator. That really intrigued me; I could only imagine the things he had seen in his life.

When Frankie and I visited with Daniel he spoke very few words. But one day as I put Frankie in Daniel's lap he cupped his hands around Frankie's face and looking into her eyes he said, "You're so special, Frankie."

"Thank you, Daniel," I said.

He looked over at me, and with tears in his eyes said, "I feel so sorry for her."

"Daniel, you don't need to feel sorry for Frankie. She's really happy and she enjoys visiting with you."

With a puzzled look, he said, "She does?"

I nodded.

His voice cracking he said, "Frankie is perfect, unlike me. I'm not perfect."

My heart broke hearing him say those words. I said, "Oh, Daniel, we think you are perfect just the way you are."

He looked back down at Frankie, and stroking her head, he smiled.

As we continued to visit Daniel I noticed that he was declining quite rapidly. Because of health regulatory issues I wasn't allowed to know what the residents' particular diagnoses were, but I could tell Daniel was not himself. As I was leaving one day I expressed my concern to Patty, who could only tell me that Daniel would likely not be with us much longer. I got in the car and cried. Frankie and I had formed a special bond with him. He was the inspiration behind my deciding to write another children's book; this one would be about Frankie becoming a therapy dog and her work at Libby's House. I thought about how I missed my own grandparents. How I wished I had spent more time with them. I felt the need to write a book that would help children understand the elderly in their own lives. I wanted to encourage them to cherish moments with their own grandparents. I also hoped through Frankie's example it would show children that despite having challenges, we can each find a way to give back to our own communities. I began working on my new book, and in January of 2009 my friend Julie delivered a beautiful little girl, whom she named Lyla.

As I continued working on my new children's book, I wrote about another resident Frankie and I had grown fond of. Susie is ninety-six years old. She has a hard time communicating and makes gibberish sounds in an attempt to let you know her thoughts. But no words are necessary when Frankie visits. The minute she sees Frankie roll into the living room, she smiles from ear to ear and begins to clap and giggle. One thing she says, over and over, is the word little. She says this as she looks at Frankie.

When my book was complete, I met with Julie and Lyla for lunch in January 2010. Lyla would soon have her first birthday. I took out two copies of my new book from my bag, and said, "Julie, this is my new book. I wanted you to know that I named one of the characters in the story after Lyla."

"Oh, that is so sweet, Barb. Which character?"

"Susie, a resident at Libby's house. She is such a sweet lady that I decided to name her after your daughter."

"I'm so touched."

"It seemed fitting to me because you were part of making my dream come true in helping Frankie become a therapy dog. And the fact you became pregnant while you were training us is so special. It is an honor to have named one of the characters after your sweet daughter."

We hugged each other while Lyla happily ate her lunch. I signed a copy of *Frankie the Walk 'N Roll Dog Visits Libby's House* to each of them as a special keepsake of our friendship.

CHAPTER TWENTY

The Gift of Jackson

About a month after Frankie and I began volunteering at Libby's House, I received a phone call from a friend named LuAnn. She does therapy dog work with her dog, Sophie, at Sharon S. Richardson Community Hospice (SSRCH). I've known LuAnn since I was a young teenager and our paths had often connected after we were adults. She supported me in my work as a new author, carrying copies of my first book with her and telling everyone she met about Frankie. She personally hand-sold my books to people she met through her work. She had heard that Frankie and I were now a therapy dog team.

She said, "There is this adorable older woman whose husband just passed away at hospice. Before her husband passed on, I told them about Frankie and gave them your book to read. The elderly woman read Frankie's book to her dying husband a few evenings before he passed."

The sweet image of this gave me goose bumps and touched me deeply.

"She would really like to meet Frankie. I hope you don't mind, but I told her that I might be able to arrange it."

I was hesitant at first. "I'm not so sure I can do that, LuAnn. I don't think I'm ready for a hospice situation. It scares me."

"I understand, and if you think you can't, I will respect that."

She told me more about the grieving widow and the more she talked, the more I wanted to at least give it a try. LuAnn said the woman would be leaving hospice in the next day or two to return home, so we didn't have much time.

I said, "Okay, I'd like to give it a try."

We made arrangements for Frankie and me to visit the next morning.

SSRCH opened in 2007 and is a state-of-the-art facility. As I drove down the long winding driveway that morning I had butterflies in my stomach. I really didn't know what to expect. I was nervous thinking about the people who have only months, weeks, or perhaps days to live. The only person I had ever seen in the dying process was my Grandpa R, many years ago. That image was still fresh in my mind and hard for me to think about.

As I parked my car, having Frankie with me made me feel braver. The thought that we would likely be a bright spot in the newly widowed woman's day made it easier too. I took Frankie out of her dog car seat. It was early fall and the grounds were in full autumn bloom as I strapped her into her wheelchair and we headed toward the front door. There was a warm breeze blowing and I couldn't help but feel a peace and calm come over me as Frankie walked beside me. SSR is on a large piece of land with a lot of open space and wildlife such as deer and turkeys. Beautiful gardens surround the property, which is maintained by volunteers.

LuAnn greeted us as we walked through the door. The inside was just as beautiful as the outside. I no longer felt nervous and almost felt serene. This struck me as somewhat odd being that I was in a place where people were spending the last days of their lives. I expected it to feel very sad. But instead, I felt serenity and warmth surrounding me.

LuAnn walked me and Frankie down the hallway to the elderly woman's room. On our way to her room, LuAnn said, "The woman's name is Lillian. I told Lillian that I have a surprise for her. She is very excited about her surprise and is curious as to what it could be." We looked at each other and smiled.

When we got to the end of the hallway Frankie was not hesitant about rolling right through the open door. I saw Lillian sitting quietly, staring out into the open field. She seemed lost in deep thought and had a smile on her face.

LuAnn said, "Lillian, I brought you your surprise." Lillian, still smiling turned her head slowly towards LuAnn. Pointing down to Frankie, LuAnn said, "Look, Lillian. I brought Frankie to meet you."

Lillian clasped her hands in front of her chest and said, "Oh, I can't believe it! I just read about you and here you are coming to visit me." She bent forward and said, "Come here, sweet one, so I can pet you."

I helped navigate Frankie towards Lillian. With my help, Frankie rolled on over and settled in by Lillian's feet. She stroked Frankie's head over and over, smiling and with tears pooling in her eyes.

Lillian said, "I can't believe that I am actually meeting the real Frankie."

"I'm so glad to know that Frankie made your day, Lillian."

"I just read Frankie's story to my husband a few nights ago. It's such a sweet story."

"Thank you. I'm so happy you enjoyed it."

Lillian kept petting Frankie and saying that she just couldn't believe Frankie was in her room visiting her. My heart was overwhelmed with joy at what had seemed a small gesture on my part meant so much to this grieving woman.

I got all choked up, looked at LuAnn, and whispered, "Thank you."

We visited with Lillian for about twenty minutes before the nurse came in with Lillian's lunch. She was having her last meal at SSRCH before heading back to her home that afternoon. I got up and gathered my coat and headed toward the door. "It was such an honor to have visited with you today, Lillian."

"Thank you so much. You really made my day."

Patting her arm I said, "You are so welcome."

LuAnn walked us back to the front of the building. I hugged her and said, "Thank you once again for the wonderful experience."

As I made my way out to the car, Frankie rolling happily beside me, I knew I'd be back. Watching Frankie jubilantly walk through the hospice halls ready to share joy and love, gave me the confidence to know I could do this too.

Volunteering in hospice requires more training than what I had to do for Libby's House. I took a full day of training in order to learn about health regulatory and safety issues, our role as a therapy dog team, and most importantly, respecting the needs and differences of all hospice patients. One of the biggest things I learned in hospice is that when I visit, I'm there for the patients. We are to leave our own worries and problems at the front door. We are not to share our personal views about dying or death, but to be there to listen. It's also not our place to judge patient's views of dying or anything else, for that matter. As I went through the training, I couldn't help but think how Frankie seemed to already know all of this. Dogs just seem to have this knowing about so much in life.

It took me a few weeks to feel completely comfortable when visiting patients with Frankie at hospice. It wasn't always easy knocking on a door, not knowing what I would find. On one of my earlier visits I was told by the receptionist that an elderly woman who had just arrived two days before would love a visit from a dog. She told me the patient was in room four. I wasn't too nervous since the patient had requested a visit from a dog; so, I had no apprehension about knocking on the door to see an elderly woman.

As I walked into the room, there was a teenage girl sitting on the sofa. She half smiled when she saw Frankie and me. At first, I wasn't able to see the patient because of a wall to the left. The blinds were also drawn so it was somewhat dark. As we got further into the room, I came around the corner and saw a middle-aged woman sitting on the bed. She was intently looking at the man lying in bed. I looked to the person in bed, but wasn't quite sure what I was seeing. I looked at the woman on the bed and said, "I was told that you requested a visit from a therapy dog?" But as the words came out of my mouth, I realized we had walked into the wrong room. This patient was in the dying process.

As the grieving woman shook her head *no,* I said, "I am so sorry. I must have misunderstood which room it was we were to visit." I quickly walked Frankie out of the room. As I came out the door, the volunteer coordinator, Betty came around the corner.

"Oh, Betty, I feel so horrible! We walked into the wrong room. It was apparent this was a very private moment between a husband and wife."

Betty put her hands on my shoulders and gently said, "Please don't feel bad. These things happen. It's okay."

Still shaken, but wanting to visit the elderly woman who had requested a visit, I followed Betty down the hall to the correct room. Her name was Ruth. She was excited to meet Frankie. As Frankie sat at her feet she told me about her family and how she told them she was ready to move on.

She said, "I'm not afraid to die."

I listened to her intently and was struck by her complete calm and the fact she had no fear of dying. A few moments later, she said she was tired. I said goodbye and Frankie and I left her alone to rest.

My heart was heavy as I drove home that day. I realized when leaving the room we had accidentally entered, that the woman sitting on the bed looked familiar to me. I remembered working with her years before at Kohl's Department Store. I didn't know her well but recalled her working in the men's department. I couldn't shake how awful I felt for walking in on what I thought might have been her last moments with her husband. The next day I read in the obituaries that the man whose room I had accidentally entered had passed away. It only made me feel worse to know that Frankie and I had interrupted what appeared a special moment between him and his wife just hours before he died.

Two weeks later, still feeling odd about my previous visit, I returned to hospice with Frankie. As we were walking to the front door I was thinking about the young girl sitting on the sofa in the room I had accidentally walked into. I thought about how she had smiled when she saw Frankie. I realized that maybe it was not accidental we walked into her dad's room when we did. Maybe Frankie was just what she needed at that moment. I felt a big weight lift off my shoulders.

As Frankie and I continued visiting SSRCH, I began telling family and friends about our hospice work. Many told me they couldn't work or volunteer in a hospice facility. The perception that many have, as I did for many years, is that it's depressing. Some people even said, "Why would you want to surround yourself with people who are dying?"

I understand their feelings, because I was apprehensive at the beginning too. But through my training and my visits, I came to realize that even though people in hospice have limited days, they are still *living*. Each time I visit with a patient, I leave with a whole new perspective on life again. It sounds cliché, but life *is* truly short. We waste so much time worrying about the little things and believe me I have wasted plenty of time worrying about small things— but I am reminded every time I walk through the front doors of hospice how precious and fragile each and every day is. It's a welcome reminder to not take life for granted. I feel very honored and privileged to share last moments or days with those whom Frankie and I visit. Also, if there are family members visiting with their loved ones they often welcome the presence of an animal in the room to help ease some of the stress and sadness they are dealing with.

Being a hospice volunteer was challenging at the beginning, but I've come to enjoy my work there, as well as the chance to put my worries aside. At first it was a challenge to get out of my own way and realize that for this one hour of volunteering, it's not about me. It's about what Frankie and I can do for the patients. It may be to listen, offer a hug, hold a hand, or just sit in silence—which is a challenge in itself. But, Frankie gave me the confidence to do this selfless work. Her willingness to walk into a room and bring joy to those in great need and those that she doesn't even know is an incredible lesson of not judging, and in giving back without wanting anything in return.

There are many sad times such as when a patient we have come to know passes away. But my life has been enriched because I know Frankie and I made a small difference in the life of that person. To be a part of patients' last days and welcomed into their rooms to offer whatever support we can, is a treasured gift, each and every time.

There is no doubt in my mind that Frankie has helped me to become a more compassionate person through our therapy dog work. I've been asked often to share my story with local organizations. In part of my talk, I share with the audience that there isn't a day goes by that I don't thank God for the gift of Frankie. She is my daily reminder to continue to think positive and look for the blessings in every challenge, no matter how difficult that challenge is.

One of the greatest gifts Frankie has given me was the opportunity to meet a very special family in December 2008. John, Frankie, and I were supposed to travel to Grayslake, Illinois for a fundraising event for Dodgerslist. They invited me to do a reading and book signing at their upcoming event. I was honored to have been asked and told them I would donate a portion of book sales to them. I was happy to do this because they had helped me greatly at the beginning of Frankie's IVDD diagnoses. The event was being held the Sunday before Christmas. The night before the winds howled and the temps dipped to thirty degrees below zero. The frigid weather was expected to last through Monday. As I checked my e-mail for the last time that afternoon a message was waiting from the event organizer. Due to an illness she had, and the inclement weather, the event was being postponed. Though I was happy we didn't have to travel in the treacherous weather, I was also disappointed. I had been looking forward to this for weeks. A few days later, Christmas was here. That afternoon, John and

I sat at our computers, checking our e-mails. A message appeared that would reaffirm for me one of my belief's which is "everything happens for a reason." It was a touching note from a mom about her special son Jackson:

> *"We bought your book a few weeks ago at the gift shop at the Osthoff Resort. Then we ran into you and Frankie at a bookstore in a town near the resort. We bought the book because my son has Hemiplegia, which is a form of Cerebral Palsy. He needs to wear braces on his legs and recently he got a new brace for one of his legs to wear at night.*
>
> *We read him your book before he got his new brace to help him accept it. As you can imagine, he very much dislikes having to wear these as they are likely uncomfortable. He is only three so it's hard to explain the reason of the value of wearing the brace. Tonight is the first night he is wearing it to bed. Your book and Frankie have helped him accept wearing his brace tremendously. Before Jackson went to bed he said, "I have to wear my brace like Frankie."*

Jackson's mom, Dawn, asked if we would be in the Chicago area anytime soon because Jackson really wanted to meet Frankie. As I printed off the letter and handed it to John I knew without a doubt Frankie was meant to meet Jackson. I believed this was part of the reason our event was postponed. As John finished reading, his eyes misted with tears. "We will be in that area on Sunday!" he said. "Jackson and his family live only twenty-five minutes from Central Bark where the Dodgerslist event was being held."

The event was nice and I enjoyed meeting everyone in person that I had been corresponding with via email through Dodgerslist. But my heart was eager to meet our new friend, Jackson. As the event ended, John helped me pack up my things and we headed to the main part of Central Bark, where we agreed to meet Jackson and his family.

A few minutes after 2 p.m., a blond boy with lots of energy and a smile as big as Texas came rambling through the front door. He may have a challenge with Cerebral Palsy, but you wouldn't know it. He was ecstatic to see Frankie! As he bent down to pet Frankie on the back, he looked up at me with his sky blue eyes and deep dimples and handed me a special doggie donut he had brought for her. He was then eager to take Frankie's leash, reaching for it, so I handed it to him. He jubilantly bounced away, holding Frankie's leash proudly. He had also brought Frankie a little stuffed toy frog, and took great delight in throwing it for her to retrieve.

As Jackson and Frankie played, Dawn showed me the night brace Jackson has to wear. She said, "Can Frankie sign it?"

It took everything I had within me to keep from crying. I was so touched. With a little help from me, Frankie inscribed Jackson's brace, "Keep on rolling!" I also gave Jackson a framed photo of Frankie and said, "This is to remind you that you can do anything you set your mind to do—just like Frankie."

Meeting Jackson was meant to be, and I'm so honored that through Frankie's story, we had the privilege to meet this sweet, young boy with a bright future ahead of him. Jackson's joy and enthusiasm is contagious. I have no doubt he will bring a positive message to our world as he grows up.

The following morning I received another email from Dawn:

> *"I just want to thank you again for giving Jackson the chance to meet you and Frankie. He is still talking about it! I apologize for being a bit late. Jackson had a hard time deciding on the perfect things to bring Frankie. The last two nights he has put his brace on easily and he seems to enjoy being "like Frankie," as he says that each time we put the brace on. He has asked me to read your book several times since meeting you both. Frankie's picture now has a very special place next to Jackson's bed. He loves to look at it and touch her. Thank you for giving that to us, it's a very special gift."*

I wiped away the tears as I bent down to pick up Frankie who was lying next to me. I hugged her tight and said, "Thank you, Frankie. I love you so much."

Dawn and I kept in touch via email, as well as a visit when she returned to my small town a year later with her sister.

Almost two years after meeting Jackson, I received another email from Dawn. Jackson was turning five in November. Dawn was having a birthday party for him. She told me she was planning the list of who to invite and had asked Jackson, "Who would you like to come to your birthday party?" Without hesitating Jackson said, "Barb and Frankie!"

I smiled as I read the email. It was amazing, the connection Jackson still had with Frankie, even though it had been two years since they met. Dawn wrote, "I know you have a very busy schedule and it's quite a distance to travel, but if there is any way you could make it to Jackson's party, I know he would love it." I checked my calendar, happy to see that we didn't have an event the day of Jackson's birthday. I emailed Dawn back and said we would be there. Dawn and I agreed it would be fun to make it a surprise and not tell Jackson that Frankie would be there. He also wouldn't be disappointed if for some reason I had to cancel. The day couldn't come fast enough. I don't know who was more excited— Dawn or me.

The day finally arrived! Frankie and I made the three-hour trip to Illinois. When we entered the parking lot of the gymnastics facility where the party was being held, I called Dawn on my cell phone to let her know we had arrived. She came outside to meet us. After an exchange of warm hugs, I gave her my video camera, which she planned to give to her sister, Lori, to record the special moment.

I said, "We will be there in a few minutes."

I carried Frankie to the front door and placed her in her doggie wheelchair. I also brought along her birthday hat which I had made for her a few years earlier. I placed it on her head and said, "Come on, Frankie. Let's go surprise Jackson!" It was as if she knew she was on a very special mission. She jubilantly pranced to the front door, her head bobbing back and forth, and her ears blowing in the wind.

As we made our way through the door, I saw Jackson sitting on his mom's lap. Lori was off to the right filming our entrance. Dawn had blindfolded Jackson to add to the surprise. As Frankie rolled up to Jackson, Dawn said, "Jackson, someone special is here to see you. Can you guess who it is?" She took his hand and placed it on Frankie's head.

Jackson enthusiastically said, "Frankie!" He ripped the scarf from his eyes to see his best pal.

I said, "Jackson, how did you know it was Frankie?"

"It felt like her."

Well, of course it did, I thought. I grinned at the simplicity of Jackson's answer.

Jackson played with Frankie for awhile and then went off to tumble, twirl, and play with the other kids. When it was time for Frankie and me to head back home, I asked Jackson if I could get a picture of him with Frankie. He sat down next to her and smiled, putting his arm around her. He then leaned over and kissed Frankie on the top of her head. It was a very tender moment. One I will never forget.

I hugged Dawn goodbye and she thanked me again for being there for Jackson. I smiled and said, "You are more than welcome."

As Frankie and I headed back home, I couldn't stop thinking about how wonderful it was that we met Jackson two years earlier, and how he continues to be a part of our lives. He has a very special place in my heart.

I thought back to the early years of my marriage and how I had felt like an outcast for not wanting children. My eyes welled with tears as I was reminded once again that we each have a purpose. I could feel in my heart that without a doubt, the children Frankie and I have encountered is all part of a Divine plan. If I would have given into societal pressures and had children, my life would have played out quite differently. As I looked back on my life, I believe my life plan was to unfold just as it has.

Dawn emailed me two days later to tell me that on their way home after the party Jackson said, "I really loved Frankie being my surprise. I'm going to miss her." She also shared with me that later that day, as he was trying on his "I Love Frankie the Walk 'N Roll Dog" sweatshirt we gave him for his birthday gift, his dog, Chance, began sniffing it. Jackson looked at Chance and said, "Frankie is *my* dog!" No doubt that Jackson and Frankie have a special connection.

CHAPTER TWENTY-ONE

Keeping the Faith

Frankie and I continued doing appearances at schools, libraries, and organizations in Wisconsin and have done close to 350 visits. I've also embraced technology and we have met many more children to share Frankie's inspirational lessons via Skype.

In the beginning, after my book was published, Frankie and I were doing two to three appearances per week, plus our therapy dog work three times a month. I was having the time of my life. It brought me immense joy. But lurking in the back of my mind was the worry about the day when Frankie would no longer be here. At times it would consume me with dread and worry. I believed with all my heart this is what God meant for me and Frankie to do. But I couldn't help but think about what path would be ahead for me when Frankie passes on. At times I made myself so sick with worry about this, that I didn't like living in my own head. I didn't want to constantly think about Frankie dying and I was tired of the constant battle in my head and telling myself not to worry. I was trying hard to live in the moment of each precious day that we had together. I was often gently reminding myself. After all, it was one of the biggest lessons I learned not only from Frankie, but Cassie, as well.

At one of our last school appearances for the year in 2010, Frankie became sick and vomited during the presentation. Luckily, I realized she was going to get sick, so I was able to place her out of sight of the audience, and grab a plastic bag. I was so sick with worry that I had a hard time proceeding with my presentation. But I was near the end of my talk, so I carried on. I could hardly wait to be done and get Frankie home.

As I drove home that day my mind was flooded with worry. I looked at Frankie and said, "What's wrong, girl?" I felt the same sensation I had when I found out that I couldn't save Cassie. As I was driving, it felt like everything was closing in around me and it felt like black walls were coming in around me. I was so stressed out I couldn't think straight. I was first and foremost worried about Frankie, but I also worried that my work with Frankie, that I had come to love with all my heart, was coming to an end. *Did Frankie get sick because she was feeling stressed out?*

When I got home I was beside myself. I wanted to jump out of my skin. I didn't know what to think or do. I called a friend telling her about Frankie's recent trembling and then getting sick earlier that day. She helped to calm me down so we could think this through. I felt in my heart and gut that Frankie was trying to tell me she wanted to slow down. She was almost eleven years old. Maybe all those appearances were getting to be too much for her. I wanted to do all I could to let her have the life she deserved, but at the same time I was absolutely devastated that I might need to slow down with her. It wasn't easy for me to accept.

A few days later I was driving to an appointment and broke down crying as I cruised down the highway. I was thinking I likely needed to change my schedule with Frankie. I remember at the beginning of our appearances, I had promised her she would always come first. I had come to really enjoy what I was doing with her, that for a time, I realized I had pushed aside what was best for her. I still feared what my future would look like when Frankie was no longer here and accepting the fact I had to limit Frankie's appearances was difficult. But I came to understand that I was being presented a new lesson to learn. I would discover that a new path for me was also trying to emerge. In order for that to happen, I had to be still and listen to what I was being shown—and most of all trust and let go.

It took me awhile to come to terms with everything. But in time, I did. I still didn't know what new direction my life was to take, but I took comfort in the fact that I finally paid attention. I also recalled earlier lessons I'd learned that we need to trust that when one door closes, a new door will open.

As spring rolled into summer, Frankie and I did a few appearances and continued our therapy dog work. In July, I noticed something wasn't right with Frankie's urine. Because I express her bladder, it's easy for me to detect when something is wrong. Her urine was cloudy and had a terrible odor. She also had been having more accidents than normal, even though I was keeping up on my schedule of expressing her. She also seemed more lethargic and didn't have as much energy as she used to. But I chalked the lethargy up to her being older. From my research on the Internet, and the fact that she is an IVDD dog, I suspected she may have a bladder infection. This is common in IVDD dogs, but she had never had one before. After taking a urine sample to the vet, a vet technician called to confirm my suspicion. Frankie did indeed have a bladder infection. She was put on antibiotics and within two days was doing much better. I was relieved.

A month later she had another bladder infection. I took in another sample, as well as scheduled an appointment with the vet. Our regular vet, Dr. B wasn't in that day, so we saw Dr. C. She weighed Frankie and was alarmed when the scale read ten pounds. Dr. C checked her records. "Eight months ago Frankie's weighed 13.8 pounds. I'm concerned about the weight she has lost."

"Well, I have her on a special new diet, which I learned about through a holistic consultant."

"I can't tell you what to do in terms of feeding her, but I would suggest you consider a new diet because it isn't good that Frankie has lost so much weight."

"I do feel comfortable with the diet because the consultant's recommendations are from a book written by a vet."

"Has the consultant personally seen Frankie since being on this new diet?"

"No."

"I can't tell you what to do. Frankie is your dog, but I am very concerned with the weight loss."

She prescribed another round of antibiotics. The bladder infection cleared up once again.

After our visit I thought more about what the vet said, but I didn't want to give into fear. I truly believed I was doing the right thing for Frankie by feeding her this new diet.

In September, Frankie had yet another bladder infection. Now I was really beginning to think this was something more serious. I tried to hide my feelings as I took Frankie to the vet clinic once again. This time the vet technician that brought us to the exam room is someone I have known for many years, and she has become a good friend. The minute we got into the exam room, I broke down crying. "I just want to get to the bottom of what is happening with Frankie. I'm so scared."

She hugged me and said, "We will do our best to help figure things out."

Dr. B was on call that day, which I was thankful for, since he is Frankie's regular vet. He went through a series of questions with me and then took Frankie to the back room to extract urine directly from her bladder. He wanted to make sure we were dealing with another bladder infection, though we were both sure we were.

When he came back he said, "While I was taking urine from Frankie's bladder she had a bowel movement."

With a puzzled look he continued, "How long has Frankie's bowels been that soft?"

"Well, pretty much since I started her on her new diet in spring."

"How often does she have a bowel movement?"

"Honestly, she seems to always be going. But, I thought it was because of her new diet."

"The amount of fecal matter that came out of her is not normal."

As we talked about what causes bladder infections, which is typically fecal matter getting into the vulva, it all made sense. Frankie was having so many more bowel movements than usual. If she was in her kennel, and I was gone, she would be sitting in fecal matter when I returned home. It was as if a light bulb finally went on in my head. It made sense why she was getting so many bladder infections.

We again talked about her diet and he felt that I should reconsider what I was feeding her. He stated again that her stool being that soft, and the amount that came out of her wasn't normal. It also began to explain in my mind, why she had lost the weight she did. The particular diet I had Frankie on had worked for other dogs, so I tried not to beat myself up for what I thought was doing my best for her. Though it would take me some time to get past the guilt of not realizing what was happening at the time. But I knew in my heart I was doing what I thought was best.

After more research, I decided on a new diet for Frankie. Within just a few short days Frankie was a new dog. Her energy returned, and her bowel movements were normal again. She was now going twice a day instead of multiple times a day. She also hasn't had another bladder infection since then. Her weight, which I closely monitored as I put her on a new diet, returned to a little over thirteen pounds, which is ideal for her frame and size.

When I look back and am honest with myself, it's fear that I let consume me—fear of Frankie dying. While I always want to do the best thing for her, I had to accept that she will eventually pass away.

I was also reminded of when Frankie was first diagnosed with IVDD, and how I believed that that there was no other option but for her to walk on her own two back legs again. I also remembered being so overwhelmed with guilt and worry. I'd constantly question if I was doing enough. I exhausted myself with research on what it was that might be the "magic bullet" to make her walk again. But, I believe now that the end result, even if I had all the resources and money to help her, may have likely been the same.

Going through everything I have with Frankie, I've come to an acceptance and peace that Frankie will one day leave me. But I've come to trust and appreciate that when the time comes I will be guided in a new direction. I also realize I will never be truly ready to say goodbye to her— but Frankie has taught me to trust and allow life to unfold one day at a time.

With Frankie feeling better, our appearances were going more smoothly again. I did make some adjustments as she still seemed to be nervous in large crowds. I now hold her in a pink pouch made especially for dachshunds, which I place over my shoulder. She fits comfortably in the front pouch pocket. It is sort of like the way a mom holds her newborn baby in a baby sling. It has turned into another lesson for children. I share with them that as we get older sometimes people and dogs like more peace and quiet, and how we sometimes need our own space. I let them know that Frankie gets nervous in big crowds, so the pouch is her safe place. I tell them it's sort of like I am Frankie's mama kangaroo and she is my little joey. They always giggle thinking of her as a baby kangaroo.

Since embarking on my journey with Frankie in 2008, so much has happened in the world. Our economy took a traumatic nose dive. At times, I feared I wouldn't be able to continue my work with Frankie because of it. While I was making money selling my books and doing appearances, it wasn't enough to add to our household income. Everything I made, I turned back into marketing to continue sharing Frankie's message. I also donate a portion of my proceeds to various charities and organizations that care for special needs pets. John's construction business was struggling because of the downturn in the economy, as many small businesses were. With so many people out of work, new home building virtually came to a standstill in our county. There were only eighty new homes built in our county in 2009; it had been double that in 2008, and triple that in 2007. Though John's company mainly did remodeling, the economy still took a toll on his business.

The years 2009 and 2010 had us living very frugally. Our Wednesday date nights stopped for a time. And as I share this, I know there were many people devastated way beyond what John and I were; my heart breaks knowing the devastation and loss others have endured. Giving up date nights isn't that much of a sacrifice when compared to people losing their homes and jobs. Many people were in over their head, and reports came out about the banks giving loans to unqualified borrowers; on the other hand, people were taking the loans even though they knew they really shouldn't be borrowing that amount of money. All of this had a ripple effect on businesses and some people were caught in the cycle. Some who had barely been making ends meet lost their jobs due to the faltering economy. John and I had begun cutting expenses and looked at the way we spent money years before when I left my full time job. Now we were cutting expenses even more. We didn't want to lose our business, or possibly our home. Fear lurked in the back of our minds, though I tried really hard not to play into that fear. I accepted reality, but I've also come to believe we can choose our thoughts. Listening to the media coverage is not something I engage in on a regular basis, because it bothers me; I am very sensitive to it. John on the other hand, says he can listen to it and it helps him gauge the future and how to move with the times for his business.

The winter of 2010 was difficult—not only financially, but weather-wise with many snow storms—and we were praying that spring would hold new promise for more construction work. I also prayed that I could continue my work with Frankie. School and library budgets were being cut. I worried whether or not Frankie and I would still get booked for appearances. Every time I let fear into my heart, I'd look at Frankie and it would help me find my way back to trusting that my work with her is my calling right now. I'd remind myself of the trust I had come to build not only in myself, but in my faith. I believed we would be provided with answers and resources. I had to keep following my heart.

Spring and early summer continued to be slow and construction jobs were limited. John was used to remodeling jobs of $40,000 to $60,000, but those had become far and few between. Homeowners were choosing smaller jobs like new roofs, windows, and doors. John continued to adjust his overhead expenses and I did what I could to clip coupons and shop frugally. Fall continued in the same pattern as spring and summer. With winter approaching, John was becoming very concerned, though I didn't realize the full extent of his concerns at the time.

During winter we hunkered down and tried to stay upbeat and positive, believing everything would eventually shake out. For our weekend entertainment, John and I played Yahtzee. With our dogs snuggled into their beds, John and I would get lost in playing games at our kitchen table, while dinner was baking in the oven. When I think about those weekends, I see that although we were scared about the future, they were some of the best and coziest times. Our love for our dogs and one another deepened, as well as our gratefulness for what we did have. We'd often sit in conversation, sharing our appreciation for the simple things in life and the simple moments.

With the release of my second children's book in January 2010, I kept busy with marketing and booking school and library appearances. That focus helped keep me positive. Every time we'd visit a school and I'd meet children so excited to meet Frankie, it gave me much hope for our future. However, with people struggling because of the economy, book sales became a bit harder to come by when visiting schools. Though this was difficult, I understood families were trying to make ends meet, just like we were. Many schools we visited were classified as Title 1 schools, which meant many of the kids come from low-income households. Of course, as an author, I want to sell books; not only because it's income for me, but because I love the idea of children having a copy of my book in their little hands to treasure. But even if book sales were low, I knew in my heart I still wanted to do what I could to make an impact on children's lives. Sharing Frankie with kids who come from struggling homes–whether from financial woes, alcoholism, or abuse–made me want to share Frankie's positive story even more. I wanted to help these kids see that they could do anything they set their minds to, despite their circumstances. Even if it meant fewer book sales, and it meant not getting my full appearance fee, I was willing to work with each school or library.

The end of March meant spring was just around the corner again. Though I tried to stay positive in regards to John's business, I could see a change in him that concerned me greatly. He didn't always share financial worries with me, partly because I've always trusted him, and partly because it's not something I've always dealt with easily. But John seemed to have a shorter fuse than usual. Things set him off easily, which wasn't at all like him; he has always been an optimistic and positive person. The year before, we had turned to our financial consultant, asking for advice on how to ride out the down economy—we had our own ideas, but we were advised to just hold on. So we did. As the stock market continued to fluctuate drastically, and the economy didn't improve, I really started to worry. I felt myself struggling with keeping my faith. John was struggling too, and rightly so, because he has always carried the majority of the responsibility when it came to our household finances. I was still worried about the future, but also believed John and I could get through anything.

I've always felt incredibly blessed for the relationship I have with John. Conversation flows easily, and laughter is abundant in our home. He often makes me laugh; I love that about him. Another thing I love about him is the understanding and love he has shown to me in supporting my work with Frankie. It wasn't easy for him in the beginning, when Frankie was diagnosed with IVDD. So much of my attention was given to caring for her. Then when I decided to pursue sharing her story, he believed in me and gave me the space to follow my heart. I've come to see in John a new compassion for many things in life, not just because of what Frankie has taught me, but from what *he* has learned from her. He also sees me living from and following my heart, which in turn makes him happy. John and I have often discussed how stressed out I was when I was working in the corporate world, and how that affected our marriage. Now that I was living more authentically, I was rarely stressed out and I was able to be there not only for myself and my dogs, but for John as well.

You will often hear John say we are the "Techel Team." He supports me in my decisions, and I support him in his. I try to be his sounding board when he is struggling with business issues. In the past, when my mind was full of my own work stresses, I couldn't find the energy to listen to him. Truly being there for one another and listening to each other, we believe has helped us to not only make our marriage stronger, but has helped us to weather the storm the last few years.

It was one of those days when the hint of spring was in the air that I decided to venture out with Kylie to the back garage, which John has dubbed as his "man shed." John was out there puttering around, and I was feeling eager to get some fresh air and just hang out with John, even if it meant being in the man shed. When I opened the side door and looked in, I didn't see him at first. But as I looked around again, I saw him in the far back corner of the garage. He looked startled to see me, and his face seemed to drain of color. He made his way from the back of the garage, with the strangest look still on his face. I felt like maybe I had "caught him" at something. My heart began to race.

Trying not to jump to conclusions I said, "What were you doing?"

Somewhat defensive, he said, "Nothing."

"Then why do you have that funny look on your face?"

"I don't have a funny look on my face."

"What were you doing back there?"

"Nothing."

By now my mind was really racing with thoughts of what he could have been doing. *A woman's worst nightmare,* I thought. *Was he on his cell phone with a mistress?* I have always trusted John, but I couldn't help my mind from thinking it. Trying to dismiss that thought, I said, "Are you hiding something back there?"

"No."

"I'm going to walk back there."

"Go ahead."

I felt bad for not trusting him, but yet I knew something wasn't right. I made my way to the back of the garage and looked around, and felt relieved that everything seemed as it should be. Walking back to the front of the garage John still didn't seem himself. I decided not to push it any further as I could see he was really agitated. I said, "I don't know why you seem so different, but I'm going back to my writing cottage. I just came out here because I wanted to be with you."

I walked away and headed back to my cottage. I was still somewhat shaken by something that I couldn't identify and truly felt something was amiss. A few moments later, John came into my cottage, holding a piece of paper in his hand. He handed it to me, and sat down in the chair across from me.

Before looking at it, I said, "What is this?"

"Just read it."

It was an email he had put together for our financial consultant, outlining his plan to make some financial choices so that we could breathe a little easier. As I finished reading it, I looked at him and said, "I totally trust you and agree with this choice."

"When you came out to the garage a few moments ago, I was trying to figure out a way to tell you this."

My heart ached greatly that this was so hard for him to do. The heavy load John had been carrying the last few years all made sense to me now. While we couldn't control the economy and the stock market, we could control our own lives and what we wanted for it. I realized John had been under a tremendous amount of stress. It just wasn't worth jeopardizing his health. The financial decision we were about to make was right for us, to help ease some of the burden. Though we may have gone against what is preached to us and what we must do in terms of money and the future, we were comfortable that this was the right decision for us.

So often I think we live in fear of the "what ifs" that we forget to live in the now. I know I certainly can fall into that trap, but have learned to be much more aware of it. Cassie was the first dog to teach me to live in the moment, and now Frankie and Kylie are my daily reminders. I'd still let fear creep back into my mind now and then wondering what people would think of our financial decision if they knew. But again I reminded myself that this was our choice, and it was right for us. And truly it was no one else's business, but ours. Trusting the Universe and all that we believe about living our dreams and following our hearts, we took what we had saved for years and paid off our home mortgage and business loans. We were then debt-free, which meant we could both continue doing what we loved and not live in fear of possibly losing our home or business. Taking the future into our own hands and not letting the unstable stock market or faltering economy overtake us with fear, we felt a huge weight lift off our shoulders. Though it wasn't easy at first to take such a big leap of faith, we knew we could only go up from here. We were excited to move forward.

I'm also reminded of the lesson Frankie taught me when I had her fitted for her wheelchair. How I feared what others would think of me that I put my dog in a wheelchair. How I worried so much for so many years what others thought of me, no matter what decisions I made. I didn't want to live in that world any longer. If our decision felt right to John and me then it didn't matter what others thought. It was our life and we had to live it the way we chose.

As the weeks began to pass, it was amazing what happened. All of a sudden John's business phone began to ring off the hook. More and more work was coming in—though we continued to hear that many contractors in our area were still not busy. As the workload increased, we thanked God every day for the blessings.

Maybe you could chalk it up to the economy coming back somewhat, but according to news reports we still had a long way to go as a nation. It was sometimes hard to escape the negative news; it was everywhere. But I choose to believe that when you make choices based on what is right for you and your life, the Universe will support you. I am reminded of following my heart back in late 2007 and writing my first children's book and how scared I was. But I chose to believe that if I did my best and followed my heart's calling, everything else would fall into place. It did. And it continues to now.

CHAPTER TWENTY-TWO

Standing Tall

It took me until my early forties to awaken and discover that I am entitled to live a joyful and authentic life, and that I always have choices. Frankie reminds me of this every day when I awake and see her happy, sweet face beside me.

As the idea started to formulate in my mind about writing this book, I felt fear return once again. I also felt myself falling back into the pattern of worrying about what others would think of me and the choices I have made. Something then occurred to me that struck my heart deeply. When I began my journey with Frankie, I found myself standing behind her as I built my confidence in who I am. As my confidence grew, I found myself standing beside her. As I contemplated writing this book to share my story, I knew I still had work to do in growing and believing in me. I know as Frankie grows older my life will change when she is no longer here and I will have to stand on my own. Just typing those words, a great feeling of sadness overcomes me, while at the same time a feeling of liberation is happening too. I know everything will be okay because I'm already standing on my own. To think a little dog on wheels taught me some of life's greatest lessons is very profound for me. But it's in moments like these that I can't seem to find the right words to adequately express how my heart feels, that I was chosen to walk this path with Frankie and learn from her as I have. I'm so incredibly grateful that God put me and Frankie together on this earth to do the work that we do.

As Frankie ages, people have begun asking me how I will go on after she is gone. At first this question bothered me immensely. Actually, I was somewhat taken aback that people would ask me such a question. The more I thought about it though, I believe that they don't mean harm by the question, but it is more out of concern for my well being.

I struggled for some time with the thought of Frankie dying and I still have my moments. It certainly will not be an easy day when I lose Frankie, and I know it will break my heart beyond words. But I also know that without loss and sadness we can't experience joy and new beginnings. Facing the fear of Frankie dying and what my future will look like certainly hasn't been easy—it has actually been quite painful for me at times. But the more I faced the fear and began to know that life will go on, I found myself being open and trusting that a new path will emerge for me when the time is right. As I finish writing the last chapter of this book, new opportunities have come to light because of learning to let go and trust. I find myself in a more peaceful place now, enjoying new avenues I am exploring, while Frankie enjoys her senior years.

In a book I read daily called, *The Book of Awakening, Having the Life You Want by Being Present to the Life You Have,* by Mark Nepo I was deeply affected in a beautiful way by the author's entry on November 22 about grief. He said, "I've learned that grief can be a slow ache that never seems to stop rising, yet as we grieve, those we love become more and more a part of who we are. In this way, grief is yet another song the heart must sing to open the gate of all there is."

Frankie has been an integral part of helping me morph into who I am. I believe when she leaves her physical body she will still be with me in spirit, and the bond between us will never be broken. I'm learning to trust in the unseen and know that our souls will always be intertwined. I remember to take several moments each day to just sit and be with her. I breathe in every part of her so that she stays with me long after I can no longer hold her soft body in my arms. I know that letting her go one day will bring another lesson in what this thing called life is all about.

I truly believe Cassie's cancer diagnoses led me to working with a life coach, to becoming a writer, to Frankie's diagnoses of IVDD, and then our work together. This is truly the path I was meant to travel to find the heart and soul of who I am—to be comfortable in my own skin and proud of who I am. I wouldn't trade any of the last ten years for anything. I've grown and evolved in ways I could have never imagined. I learned so much from Cassie, and also from Kylie, but most of my moments of truth and the opening of my spirit have come about because of my little dachshund who rolls through life on wheels. My life will never be the same because of Frankie, and for that, I am forever deeply and profoundly grateful.

Afterword

Summer lay before me as I anticipated hours of quality time with Frankie; walking her in her dog stroller, riding my bike with her as co-pilot in her basket on my handlebars, and snuggling with her to my heart's content. While I had struggled with retiring Frankie, I had come to a peaceful place with it.

We made our last appearance on Friday, June 14th, 2012. We visited a local senior community where I shared Frankie's story with those that had gathered for lunch and fellowship. At one point during my presentation, I got choked up as it hit home that this would be the last time. But soon enough I recomposed myself and finished, relishing in each last word.

As I held Frankie in my arms and walked to the car after the presentation I kissed the side of her snout over and over. "We did it Frankie! Now it is your time to rest, little one. I love you so much."

As I buckled her into her car seat I said, "We are going to have a wonderful summer- just you and me." I smiled as I thought about our new chapter of slowing down and relishing more simple pleasures.

The following morning something tugged at my heart. Something was not right with Frankie—it was something that had been nagging at me, but it was nothing consistent until the past week; a cough that Frankie had that seemed to be getting worse. I called the vet clinic and my voice was shaking. "If I can get Frankie in for an appointment today I would be grateful. Something isn't right, I just know it."

Three hours later, after a chest x-ray, she was diagnosed with chronic heart disease. I couldn't believe those were the words Dr. B spoke to me. *How could this be?* I wondered. I have the whole summer planned out for us. The thought also raced through my mind that I had hoped with all my heart that Frankie would live to be at least seventeen years old. I couldn't believe this was happening. It felt so surreal.

As I got in the car, overwhelmed with sadness, I looked at Frankie and was reminded that I had to kick into my positive mode. I had to have hope and give the medication a chance to work.

On Saturday I put Frankie in her dog stroller to rest as I planted some flowers. Like always, her eyes followed my every move. Early Sunday afternoon, just before we headed out for a family gathering, I noticed Frankie's heart rate seemed to have increased. I tried not to worry, but when we returned home a few hours later her heart rate still seemed elevated.

After a quick call to Dr. B he suggested I bring her in early Monday morning. Frankie had a restless night of tossing and turning, and I was beside myself with worry. Once at the vet, Dr. B gave her a high dose injection to try and clear the fluid off her lungs, which was making it hard for her to breathe.

On Monday and Tuesday I slept on the sofa, so as not to disturb John when I gave Frankie her 1 a.m. dose of medication. Frankie was snuggled in her bed, which I placed on the oversized chair, then pulled the chair tight against the couch so she was next to me.

While the injection seemed to help on Monday to ease Frankie's breathing, by midday on Tuesday I could tell her breathing had gotten worse again. During the night I began to sense that Frankie was beginning her transition. Every time I looked at her she had her head up, never laying it down to sleep. She also starred straight ahead as if she wasn't here.

As the first light of day peeked through the windows, I knew I needed to speak the words I never thought I'd ever be able to. I pulled Frankie next to me, cuddling her in my arms. I looked into her eyes and with all the courage I could find, I said, "If you need to move on little one, it's okay...I'll. Be. Okay...I promise."

An hour later I called the vet clinic to let them know Frankie was not doing well. The receptionist scheduled our appointment with Dr. B for 3 p.m.

Frankie and the Animal Communicator

Later that morning, I called my friend Mary. "I think I have a very tough decision to make soon, for Frankie."

Without hesitating, Mary said, "Call Dawn."

"Who's Dawn?" I didn't expect her to say that.

"She's a friend of mine and she's an animal communicator. I think she can help you."

I've had readings done in the past for Cassie, as well as for Kylie, so I was familiar with the power of what can be discovered through animal communication. But it didn't occur to me to do this with Frankie. What a gift Mary had just given me in making this suggestion.

I called Dawn as soon as I hung up with Mary. When she answered, I told her that our mutual friend Mary had referred me. I then explained my distress about Frankie. She told me she was in the middle of a big book production, but said, "I can hear in your voice that you are really struggling. Email me three recent photos of Frankie, and one recent one of the two of you. Call me back in an hour."

I made Frankie comfortable on the ottoman in my writing cottage, then I sat in my wicker chair across from her. An hour later I picked up the phone and called Dawn back. Dawn's voice answered softly, "Hi Barb."

"Hi Dawn."

"I want to share with you first what Frankie is telling me to tell you. We can then move into any questions you may have for her."

"Okay."

"Frankie told me loud and clear that you two are a team. There is a very deep love between the two of you. Frankie says that there has been an evolution of equality between the two of you. She is reaffirming that what you gave her is equal to what she gave you."

I smiled as she continued, "What I'm getting from Frankie is that she was a channel of healing energy for you—that there was much below the surface for you that needed healing."

This brought tears to my eyes because nothing could have been more true. Frankie did indeed help heal my feelings of failure and inadequacies I'd felt about myself for years.

"How old is Frankie?" Dawn asked.

"She will be thirteen on August 20th."

"Oh, well she says she feels like she is seventeen—meaning she has lived a very full life."

Hearing this actually brought me a great deal of comfort, as it had been my wish.

"Frankie doesn't want you to blame yourself for what seems so sudden with her illness. She has felt this tiredness coming on for a long time but never showed it to you because she was invested in your feelings."

More tears streamed down my cheeks to think she had done all this for me.

"She's now telling me that she really started to enjoy the presentations you did together. She said that you learned to go with the flow and she liked that. At the beginning you used to be too controlling."

I chuckled. I couldn't believe Frankie told Dawn this—this isn't something I'd ever admitted about myself or ever talked about. Public speaking is a hard thing to do and I remember how nervous I was at the beginning. I'm also an organized person which I guess can be seen as controlling, but I always wanted everything to go perfectly. As I did more speaking engagements, I learned to relax and just be me.

"Frankie says you are a real go-getter and that she often fed off of your high energy. Frankie stayed longer than she had planned, but that her life was better than she could have ever imagined."

Dawn also told me that she felt that Frankie gave me a deeper softening of my heart, helping me to not be so controlling of situations. She also said that Frankie helped deepen my compassion not only for animals, but for people as well. I absolutely agreed with that, as it was exactly how I felt, as if my heart cracked wide open because of what I learned from her.

"Things are winding down for Frankie."

Though they were words I feared hearing, I already knew this in my heart. "Frankie is floating in and out of being here on earth and wanting to move on." I could feel this as well about her.

"I don't sense a need of urgency in making a decision whether to help Frankie or she may also go on her own. But what Frankie wants is what is right for you—whatever you need."

Through the tears I knew this, too. We have such an incredibly deep bond, so how could I not know?

I thanked Dawn for dropping everything to help me. Before we hung up Dawn told me that she had done many animal readings in her life, and the connection she felt between me and Frankie was very strong. She thanked me for allowing her to be a part of Frankie's journey.

As I hung up the phone I cried like I never cried before—not only out of deep sadness, but with gratitude for being able to travel this most amazing journey with Frankie.

I've often said that I have no doubt that the past six years with Frankie, and all we did and learned together, was meant to be. Even if I do nothing else in my life, this is what I was brought here to do. I also know, although my heart felt like it would literally crumble all around me, that I did the right thing for Frankie at the end. I think too often we fear death and then we are not in the present moment of it, and we lose out on the many gifts it has to offer. I feel privileged to have witnessed many gifts near the end of Frankie's earthly journey.

With the help of Dr. B, who came to my writing cottage on June 21st, Frankie was eased into a new world. Her spirit is very much with me and the gifts continue to come.

Frankie's Visit as a Hummingbird

As I finish writing the afterword, it has been two months since Frankie passed. I continue to stay open to Frankie guiding me from the other side and share with you one last story of her recent visit to me as a hummingbird.

It was late afternoon on Saturday and I was sitting outside on the deck, listening to the radio, when one of my favorite songs came on: *Landslide* by Fleetwood Mac. It always made me think of Frankie, especially the line when Stevie Nicks sings, "Well I've been afraid of changing because I built my life around you." One of my biggest fears was that I wouldn't be able to go on after Frankie died. I had built my life around her. She was my passion, and sharing her special message of hope with others truly made my heart sing.

As I was listening to the song, a hummingbird was drinking from the feeder I have on the front of my writing cottage. My eyes filled with tears, partially out of sadness, but also from realizing that I was going on with my life without Frankie, and I was doing okay.

Just then the hummingbird swooshed over to me and was right in front of my face, fluttering its tiny wings. I was in complete awe. In all the years I've had a feeder for them a hummingbird never came that close to me. I whispered, "Frankie, is that you?"

She flitted again side to side, and then flew away. My heart oozed over with love. I smiled. I knew it just had to be Frankie.

Monday morning Frankie was in my thoughts again as I sat down at my computer to write. A moment later I saw something out of the corner of my eye. As I slowly turned my head to the right, I saw a hummingbird again, looking in the window, fluttering its little wings. I felt again that it just had to be Frankie, reminding me that her legacy continues and that it always will. And it was if she was staying to me, "Have no fear, I will always be here."

While I know not everyone will believe in such things as this, I realize how far I've come in my sharing my truth. Years ago I would have hesitated to share this story for fear of what others would think. But I know in my heart what is true for me. That is all that matters. And to think a little dog on wheels taught me this, and continues to remind me to appreciate my authenticity, is by far one of my greatest blessings.

Resources

- Eddie's Wheels: Custom-built rear wheel, front wheel quad carts for pets. Also carry a line of aids for rehabilitation equipment for vets and physical therapists, eddieswheels.com
- Dodgerslist: Organization dedicated to providing education, resources and help to those whose pets have been diagnosed with Intervertebral Disc Disease (IVDD), dodgerslist.com
- National Walk 'N Roll Dog Day: Honoring and celebrating dogs in wheelchairs who teach us to embrace each day with love, hope and joy. Founded in 2012 and celebrated every September 22, nationalwalknrolldogday.com
- Lead Your Life: Serving business leaders who want to discover who they are, decide what's important and do what matters, leadyourlife.com
- Animal Communication: Dawn Baumann Brunke, animalvoices.net
- Certified Coaching Directories: certifiedcoach.org, coachfederation.org
- Therapy Dogs Inc.: therapydogs.com

Acknowledgements

My journey in life would never be what it is had it not been, nor would this book have come to life, had it not been for my wheelie dog, Frankie. I am no longer the same person I was because of this little dog with a spirit bigger than life itself. I see, speak, and think in a new way because of her. I've also found a peace about myself I never had before. Though I miss you dearly little one, the abundant joy you brought to my world lives forever in my heart.

While I am thanking dogs, I must also thank the one who gave me the courage to try my hand at sharing my love of dogs through writing—a very special thank you to my chocolate Lab, Cassie for being my shining example that life truly is short, so get on with what is important. You too have a permanent place of love in my heart. Also a special thank you to Kylie, my English yellow Lab, who reminds me each and every day to slow down and enjoy each moment.

To my husband John, my partner, and my personal comedian who brings laughter to my life each and every day—I think we'd both have to agree that Frankie made us better people and deepened our love not only for each other, but for life itself. I love you with all my heart my dear Johnnie.

To my mom, dear friend, confidant and advisor—there are just no words to adequately touch the depth of my love for the woman who believes in me no matter what, and inspires me to be the best that I can be.

A grateful thank you to my friend, Mary Shafer, who gave me so much amazing advice and guidance all because she believes in me. It does not getter better than that.

To my editor, Yvonne Perry who took on this project even with all that she had on her plate. I'm beyond thrilled that I had your loving and gentle guidance to make this book the best it could be.

To my copyeditor, Dana Micheli for doing what she does best so I need not worry about grammar and grammatical issues and so I could just write from the heart.

Thank you to writing coach, Cynthia Morris and the Creative Leap Club which helped catapult me out of fear and into what I knew I needed and wanted to make my book a reality.

To my friend, and who I will always consider my life coach, Diane Krause-Stetson—even though we don't see each other often, the seeds that you helped plant continue to sprout and grow. I am forever grateful.

To Dawn and Jackson for being a part of my journey—what can I say except that you are two very special people.

A grateful thank you to Derek Murphy for your patience with me as we discussed the cover of my book and a special thank you to Caryn Newton for your excellent, detailed work for the interior.

To my followers on Facebook and readers of my blog who eagerly anticipated the release of this book. Thank you for your eagerness to read my story. It means the world to me.

Last, but certainly not least, to my friends and family who continue to be my teachers—I am grateful for the lessons.

About the Author

Barbara Techel is the author of the award winning *Frankie, the Walk 'N Roll Dog* children's book series. When her dachshund, Frankie, suffered a spinal injury, Barbara had her custom-fitted for a wheelchair. Frankie persevered, and Barbara realized the beautiful opportunity she had to share Frankie and give others hope and inspiration to be the best they can be. Barbara and Frankie made over 650 appearances to schools and libraries, as well as a therapy dog team routinely visiting a local senior assisted facility, hospice community and hospital.

Barbara and Frankie's story was featured in *Dogs and the Women Who Love Them: Extraordinary True Stories of Love, Healing, and Inspiration* and *Animals and the Kids Who Love Them* by Linda and Allen Anderson. Their story has also appeared in *Every Dog Has a Gift* by Rachel McPherson. Barbara has also been featured in *Woman's World, The American Dog, Doxie Digest,* and *Dog Living* magazine. Barbara's children's series have won many awards including awards from USA Book News and Dog Writer's of America.

Barbara is a passionate advocate for dogs with Intervertebral Disc Disease (IVDD) and for dogs in wheelchairs. In August 2012 she founded National Walk 'N Roll Dog Day in memory of Frankie and in honor of all dogs in wheelchairs. When not writing or blogging, Barbara loves date nights with her husband John, and spending as much time as she can with her dogs, Kylie and Joie.

- To connect with Barbara Techel visit her website (joyfulpaws.com)
- E-mail: barb@joyfulpaws.com
- Social networks: facebook.com/joyfulpaws, facebook.com/nationalwalknrolldogday, Twitter: @joyfulpaws